JONATHAN KINCAID

The New Blue: A Democrat's Roadmap to the Working Man

First edition

This book was professionally typeset on Reedsy.
Find out more at reedsy.com

Contents

Introduction

- What I am writing about and who I'm writing it for.
- Who am I to speak on this?

What has happened to the average American? It seems that the *working man* has become a mythical figure in the political discourse of today. I find myself at a crossroads wondering why the moderate majority has gone silent. All of the decision making seems to be getting pushed further and further to the fringe. Our nation is unraveling at the seams in our hour of need. Great change is on the horizon, but much uncertainty remains. The flaws of our systems have never been quite so visible, and it is readily apparent that now is the time for new beginnings. It is time to reimagine the working man and his needs.

These are truly desperate times for our country. Three-hundred thousand dead Americans and counting as the Corona-Virus Pandemic continues to wreak havoc on our health and economic well-being. In times of crisis, we come to depend upon strong leadership. Looking around it seems to be noticeably absent from our government.

The President is refusing to acknowledge the results of a free and fair election. His cabinet staff held a screaming match inside the Oval Office on this very day, where it was suggested that the President resort to martial law to remain in power. Meanwhile, in Congress, an equally disturbing saga continues to unfold. After months of failed stimulus negotiations, they now enter the weekend with a government shutdown as the deadline to appropriate more funds has lapsed. It sounds like the plot of a post-apocalyptic political thriller, but unfortunately, the nightmare is real and we are living in it.

At the time of this writing, we live in a nation that believes it is deeply divided. There is a widely held sentiment that multiple versions of the truth exist and that we live in two different Americas. I've been hearing this narrative for years and I have seen it impact every aspect of our communities. Political philosophers would call this phenomenon *constituent-sorting*, the idea that people of like-political beliefs move to be within proximity of one another, and that their beliefs become strengthened and self-reinforcing. While there is certainly evidence to support this, it is also equally probable that people who live in the same community experience similar problems and hold similar world views because of the circumstances around them.

Within the two Americas, there is a two-party political system that has become ever more polarizing. This is a product of our unfortunate "first-past-the-post" system of voting. When a candidate only needs 50.1% of the vote to win, interest groups inevitably consolidate until there are only two parties. This has devolved into the completely irrational big-tent parties of the present. Once one party has proclaimed a position on an issue, the opposing party will take the exact opposite position, regardless of the sensibility in making that decision. Figuratively speaking, it seems that we truly have been left with two Americas.

One party adopts the interests of rural citizens, and the other represents the interests of urban citizens. In order to win, they must find enough common ground with the suburban voters in between. I do not have to tell you which party is which because you already know. The very idea that you can associate their identity with this outcome presents a serious problem for a nation built around unity. We are after all the United States of America, it is in our very name. The parties that should be working together, are driving us deeper into division.

The problem begins with the incredulous number of labels that have become equated with our political parties; liberal and conservative, socialist and capitalist, communist and authoritarian, etc. Depending on the moment the label could be derogatory, or a badge of honor depending on its use. Unfortunately, any American could tell you exactly which labels to box the parties into, or at least suggest which direction they lean. These categorizations are typically flawed because these labels are used casually with reckless indifference to their academic ideology. The parties bear no resemblance to their respective labels. A careful analysis demonstrates with clarity that the parties have no consistent logical philosophy on governance and politics.

You cannot in good faith say that a Republican administration that racks up trillions of dollars in deficit spending is conservative. You also cannot say that a Democratic administration that mandated private health insurance is liberal. Spare me the labels and let us return to a time where the conversation on political issues hinged on the basis of reality. Let us talk about what things actually are instead of what they are purported to be. Then we can begin to find some common ground.

Aside from the terms Democrat and Republican, I grant you the use of one solitary concept of ideology, and that is the concept of the two freedoms. The first being the *freedom to,* and the second being the *freedom from.* As a matter of supporting individual liberty, I tend to favor the party which most endorses the *freedom to* position. I often find that *freedom from* tends to have no physical impact on the restrictor, but rather upon their sensibilities. I am of the belief that laws and governance should respect the rule of logic and reasoning. A civilized government should protect the rights of an unpopular minority to exercise their freedom as much to the extent that it does not infringe upon that of another. As such, I have historically supported the Democratic Party because I find that it is most frequently aligned with these values.

The purpose of this book is to offer up a roadmap for Democrats to rediscover the needs and desires of the *working man.* It is my goal to chart a pathway towards restoring the American middle-class and bridging the divide between urban and rural interests. America functions best through unity and it is time that we restored our commitment to the social contract. It is my hope that by the end of this book we will come to understand one another better and find opportunities for growth and compromise. This year the Democrats ran on a winning platform of *build back better.* If they are sincere in this effort, it is my hope that we can mend our divisions and emerge from this crisis with a prosperous future ahead of us. I intend to keep this more as a discussion on the merits rather than a pure exercise in academic veracity. I will provide a few inspirational accreditations at the end and you are welcome to investigate my claims and proposals for yourself. In fact, I encourage it.

Who am I to speak on this?

As this is a political text you knew that this would be provocative. Only a few pages in and I know that many of you are already prepared to pounce. Before you dismiss me as an overeducated liberal elitist, or conservative neoliberal apologist, or whatever term you may use to describe an *asshole*, let me at least explain my background first. We are not as different as you might believe and whether you are living in urban blue America, or rural red America, I see you, I know you, and I understand your point of view. My goal is to bring us together as a person split between two worlds.

I grew up in a small rural Texas town. It was sizable enough to boast having two rodeos, well perhaps a rodeo and a half as one was just for horse racing. There were only a few thousand people out there, and most of them grew corn as they had done for over a hundred years since the first grist mill was built there.

My neighborhood was among the first new suburbs to pop-up in the town, though it was still within the state of reason. The main street was only a few blocks away. It consisted of a row of about ten storefronts put up in the mid to late 1800s. You could walk down to the grocery store. You could walk to the town library. You could walk to the fire station and the police station. You could walk to the school. You could walk down to the local feed store. Everything was very local. Everyone knew everybody. Kids rode their bikes all over town. People knew their neighbors. Once a year in the fall they would close off the main street for a festival featuring hayrides, pumpkin carving, and local country artists. People drove trucks because they used them for work, and people dressed like cowboys because they actually owned cows. It was the picturesque charming rural community.

It was only a short drive to the highway and you could reach Dallas or Fort Worth in about thirty minutes. At that time there was still some noticeable separation between the two. It was through this conduit that my dad was able to support the family on a factory worker's wages. He had a great job building stealth bombers out at LTV. It came with good benefits. It afforded all of our bills and my mother was able to stay home with me as a child. One of the last of his kind, my dad worked in the same factory for decades.

Most of the families in my neighborhood were similarly situated. My neighbor down the street built cars out at General Motors. My neighbor across the street worked for a trash bag manufacturer. No one was by any stretch of the imagination rich, but they were all getting by relatively well. There was a great sense of pride in what they had built and what they had accomplished. The national consensus was that of hope for a greater tomorrow.

On the uglier side, our town was known as one of the last places in the United States to integrate their schools. A commemorative light post downtown once marked the location of the community lynching post. The Klu Klux Klan used to hold regular meetings at the local Beefers restaurant. You would think it would be a bastion of hellacious intolerance, and at one point it certainly was. However, much of this was eroded by the time of my youth.

Despite the blight of this legacy, overt racism was not as prevalent you might imagine. The working-class nature of my neighborhood lent itself to great racial diversity. Black, White, Asian, Latino, in our neighborhood it didn't matter. All the kids could play together. Our fathers all worked together at the same factories. We all attended the same churches and schools. There were a few *assholes* out there, but they were never celebrated. My next-door neighbors were a lesbian couple. They adopted a child and cashed in on the emu farming business when that trend rolled through the mid-90s. In my senior year of high school, we elected a Black prom king. The biggest conflict in town was primarily over who would be the first to get to lunch on Sundays, the Methodists or the Baptists. Call me biased, but that was a battle frequently won by the Methodists because nobody had to be *saved* and the pastor was going to cut it off at noon no matter how deep he was into the sermon.

The notion that we were some backwater hellhole of ignorance and racism would have been an egregious stereotype. Yet, I know that this is what most urban readers are thinking about small towns. There was once a time in America when the majority of small towns reflected such a robust and diverse dynamic. The stains of the Confederacy have always lingered over the South, but in those days they were steadily diminishing. The "Blue States" and "Red States" of America had far less meaning.

In Texas, we had Democratic governor Ann Richards. Bill Clinton was readily elected president across numerous Southern states. Democrats and Republicans alike would not have readily given up on any state as being unilateral. This notion that states are rigid and unchanging is a relatively new political concept, and I would argue was never true. A Republican president can lose Georgia. A Democratic president can lose Pennsylvania. The past few years have shown us just how dynamic our elections can be and should be.

My soiree into politics happened when I was in the second grade. I served as an election judge in our school's mock election. Then third-party candidate Ross Perot received the majority of the vote. My parents were both involved in the Perot Campaign. I remember going with my dad to pass out yard signs for gubernatorial candidate Democrat Martin Frost. I recall meeting Geoge Bush Jr. at a local debate. He offered me a donut.

A few years later, I attended the Democratic National Convention when my dad was a delegate. This is where I first met Jesse Jackson and then-Vice President Al Gore who was on his way to receiving the nomination. Politics was in my veins. Nothing felt quite so defeating as watching the results of the 2000 election unfold. It was around this time that my hometown took a dramatic shift for the worst.

Our local school district was rated among the top in the nation by some sort of magazine which featured such articles. The town began to explode with development. There was a great exodus from New York and California. People would sell their modest million-dollar homes in the big cities and then move out to my hometown where they would build row after row of what were fondly referred to as "McMansions". They were unsightly suburban castles that now fill the landscape here. The fields of corn and cows grew from a town of 11,000 people to a town of about 80,000 people in a matter of ten years.

The local hometown festival was replaced with a big corporate one. The local businesses could no longer afford to stay open and one by one they shut down. The residential taxes skyrocketed. Rents grew increasingly higher. Home prices doubled and then tripled. The rodeo was torn down to make way for a new school. Those of us who grew up there quickly became acquainted with the reality of the bubble we had been living in. We were no longer welcome in our own town, or at least that is how we began to feel.

My classes at school became noticeably less diverse. The churches became less about community and more about status. Every aspect of life started to become political. Did you attend the best church? Did you drive the nicest car? Did you wear the best clothes? Did you have the biggest house? Did you believe the same things that they believed? This was the price of progress. Where there was once harmony and good nature, there was now contention and competition. 9/11 only made matters worse.

It is no mystery to me why a party that aligns itself with urban interests would struggle to win over rural small-town voters. My upbringing is of course not in itself substantive enough to say that I am qualified to speak on such matters, but it does at least give me an olive branch of common ground between the voters Democrats are trying to win over.

Let us now talk about my adult life. I have a bachelor's degree in government and anthropology from the University of Texas at Austin. I have a law degree from Texas A&M. I have a master's of education in management of technical education from Texas State. I also have a post-graduate certificate in healthcare compliance from Ashworth College in Norcross, Georgia. If education is something that you value or something that you believe lends you credibility, I have a sizable helping of it on my table.

I pay a mortgage on a house in suburbia. I own a piece of land in the middle of nowhere. I've lived downtown in an apartment in a big city, and I've lived in a friend's spare bedroom. I have seen the good and the bad in every arrangement.

If you are a person who values experience, I can speak to that as well. I have worked as a high school science teacher in the public school system for approximately six years. I was a real estate agent for about five years. I once owned a small oilfield trucking company. I've produced a few of my own musical records and published a science fiction novel. I worked as a clerk in a worker's compensation firm. I once interned with the U.S. Department of Housing and Urban Development. I've worked as a technical support operator for an internet servicing company. I've stocked shelves at Target. I worked in maintenance at Six Flags. I even used to give guided tours of a nature preserve.

I also spent a few years working for the Caterpillar corporation, building diesel engines and power generators on a factory line. I know what it's like to stand on your feet for twelve hours a day, seven days a week, getting your hands dirty and turning wrenches. I might argue that at one point in time there was no one else in America that could install an oil pan on a C9 engine as quickly, effortlessly, or efficiently as me. I worked my way up the chain there into a support specialist logistics role. I was proud of what we built there.

You can put away the daggers now. It's easy to dismiss political opinions under the basis that a person doesn't understand your point of view. They don't know your upbringing. They don't know your profession. They don't have your education or your experience. Hopefully, I'm less difficult to dismiss than most people. If there should be a staple of credibility that I have missed, I do hope that you kindly suggest to me what that is such that I might obtain that.

Believe me, I understand. I get to hear about these things all the time. Everyone thinks that their problems are unique. If only someone would listen to them, they could fix it. They know what solutions are best and politicians with their same background would as well. Nothing could be further from reality.

Let me be the first to tell you that problems are universal. Problems are systemic. Solutions can and should be applied from multiple sources. A politician who has never stepped outside of their world view, or for that matter yours, will never understand how to fix a broken system. I address you then not as a citizen of Blue America or Red America, but as a person who has seen all walks of life, traversed all fifty states, and been to the edges of the Earth.

I feel then that it is my duty to lay out the groundwork for the return of the yellow-dog Democrat. If you want to start winning again in rural America, here is a map.

The Income Tax Axe: Destroyer of Wages

- No taxes on overtime wages
- Repeal the income tax and replace it with a national sales tax.
- Send out prebate checks to compensate for cost differentials and the poverty level
- Repeal payroll taxes to incentivize hiring.

There is nothing that the American factory worker hates more than income taxes and they have every right to be upset about it. In fact, I would bet that buried underneath every other political issue, this is the primary motivator for blue-collar voters. Democrats of late have been catering to this message by saying they will compel the rich to pay their fair share of taxes. Republicans seem to use tax cuts as the solution to all problems. Both parties tip the needle ever so slightly in either direction, but really they exist on the same continuum. The difficult part is getting them to see the alternatives. You don't have to tax income.

If we're going to tax income, the single most powerful message a Democrat can offer the working man is to say "no taxes on overtime wages". No words have ever sounded so sweet to the American wage earner. I ought to run for congress in Ohio on this slogan alone, I imagine I could turn out the vote. If you are working hard for America, America should be working hard for you. This promise means that you should keep the entirety of the productivity of your excess labor. As the working majority knows, the forty-hour workweek is a cosmic mythical joke. Most of their real-time earnings come from their overtime and holiday pay. For most Americans, this "extra" income is their saving grace. When they see the amount of taxes being leached out of their overtime checks, it can be incredibly disheartening. It is these moments of disappointment that ignite the Libertarian fantasies of a tax-free world.

The majority of elected officials have no idea that Americans are working fifty, sixty, seventy, eighty-hour work weeks. I can tell you that in the oilfield and in manufacturing these schedules are the norm, not the exception. As disheartening as it is to see, it's equally frustrating to labor under. Yet there are many among us who desire this level of work because they equate hard work with success and advancement. Taxing their overtime wages says that we do not value their sacrifice. Many aspects of society would be improved if we changed that policy.

That is of course if you don't just take the full step of eliminating income taxation completely. I had the opportunity to sit in on a taxation policy lecture from then-congressman John Linder, a Republican from Georgia. While I had initially expected to find disdain in every word he said, by the end of the presentation I left persuaded. He had proposed legislation known as The Fair Tax Act. It was given due consideration and even studied by the Obama administration, but it got buried and discarded somewhere along the way. I say it is time that we gave it a new look. The bill was not so far beyond help that it couldn't be hammered out in committee. I believe there is a great deal of common ground here to be realized between Democrats and Republicans if they were only willing to consider for a moment that the pendulum is swinging on the wrong track.

No matter how you slice the cake of taxation, it inevitably becomes disincentivizing. If taxes were money that citizens were readily paying with enthusiasm, they wouldn't be taxes at all, but rather civic philanthropy. When you levy a tax on a personal income, what does it incentivize? The only possible outcome is that people will make less money. Making more money leads to greater tax burdens. People thus shift aspects of their life into non-wage earning assets to shield their money from the liability of taxes.

Wages have been stagnating for decades and are only continuing to decline as more jobs are displaced by automation. It is no wonder that state and federal coffers are going broke on income taxes then. As a former business owner, I can tell you that there is great thought that goes into this. Could we pay you more cash directly into your pocket? Yes absolutely. Companies are holding back on you, and deliberately so. It is often not with malice aforethought, they really do have your best interests at heart. Direct cash payments to employees incur not only more costs on the business end in the form of increased payroll taxes but also for you as the wage earner. It's exciting to say we gave you a raise or a bonus, but if the majority of that gets eaten up in income taxes, there is little incentive for us to want to provide that type of compensation. The gains in your take-home pay would be so marginal as to feel insulting, while they're also losing more money as a business. That is why they do other things with that money like expanded benefits packages, company dinners, or stock options. Companies are fond of showcasing these values to their employees, but they are a poor substitute for real hard cash in the eyes of the workforce.

Texas likes to flaunt its no income tax policy as a driver of its economic success. If it sounds too good to be true, that's because it is. What you do not pay in income tax here, you more than makeup for in property taxes. This actually makes the taxpaying property owner worse off than they otherwise would be with an income tax. Wages are already disincentivized federally under income taxation. State taxation of wages doesn't change that. Wages in Texas are still depressed, however now the ownership of property is also adding insult to injury. For all the big talk, Texans pay just as much in taxes as Californians do. It just comes from a different asset and they have less to show for it.

If we can't tax wages and we can't tax property, what can we tax? The answer is sales in the form of a value-added tax. This can be upsetting to hear for most people. Switching to a straight sales tax model would theoretically make everything more expensive by somewhere in the magnitude of 25% or greater in some instances. Before you dismiss the idea entirely, hear me out on why this is more beneficial and why those costs are ultimately brought down in the savings actualized from simplification and consistency of application.

A VAT tax is a built-in cost that extends from the raw materials, all the way through the supply chain. What you ultimately see on the store shelf is what you pay. There is no need for the consumer to make a complex tax calculation in their head. Some economists do not believe that such a minor inconvenience would deter consumer habits, but that is only because they've never met an ordinary person. How often have you been standing in line at the grocery store and after the taxes were added to the bill had the clerk take items out of your cart? If you haven't done it personally, you've seen someone do it. A sizable portion of product removed at the register goes to waste if it cannot be safely stored or reshelved. On a macro-level most nationwide grocery chains probably don't even notice this cost, but individual store managers are extremely concerned about how this affects their sales numbers. Hence why expensive cuts of meat and cheeses are stored behind a counter, so that they can be tax priced immediately before handing it over to the consumer, so that they know whether they can afford it or not.

The VAT tax also simplifies the tax payout process. As a business owner, you no longer have to hunt through the tax codes. There is no need for a multi-volume set of tax deductions and exemptions. You can predict exactly what your tax liability will be based on your sales volume. This makes managing quarterly finances significantly easier. When you know exactly how much your taxes cost, you know exactly how much money you have to set aside for it. On a personal level independent contractors and gig-economy workers know what I am talking about. There is a phenomenon by which you either hoard money you would otherwise spend out of concern for the future uncertain value of tax liability, or you overspend and get slapped with a tax bill at the end of the year that you cannot afford to pay. Businesses face this same level of concern. Removing that caution and fear from the process encourages proper levels of investment and spending, which is beneficial to everyone.

There is a great deal of debate surrounding VAT taxes, as they have had varying levels of success around the world. Before passing such a tax in the United States, we would need to assure with certainty that this becomes the tax that replaces all other federal taxes. If we simply added it on top of existing taxes, it would absolutely be economically damaging. Similarly, if your people are thrifty consumers, it may not be the ideal tax for your nation. The United States consumes at extravagant levels, and that makes us a prime candidate for a successful VAT tax.

Consider that the most expensive things that you purchase are amortized. Imagine that the income tax is repealed. It has now been replaced by an insanely high sales tax of 40%, an extreme example, that is double the projected costs of the Fair Tax Act. It sounds grim, but the government is still getting the same amount of money they were before. Let's see how you came out though, even in this worst-case scenario. You make an "average" salary. You normally pay about 25% to income tax. You buy a new car and it costs $25,000. Let's say with your APR you end up with about a $500 monthly payment. See what it costs you before and after the change.

Figure 1-A

Year	Salary	Federal Income Tax	$25,000 Car w/Avg. APR	Amount left for everything else
1	$50,000	$12,500	$6,000	$31,500
2	$50,000	$12,500	$6,000	$31,500
3	$50,000	$12,500	$6,000	$31,500
4	$50,000	$12,500	$6,000	$31,500
5	$50,000	$12,500	$6,000	$31,500
TOTAL:	$250000	$62,500	$30,000	$157,500

Figure 1-B

Year	Salary	No Income Tax	$25,000 Car w/Avg. APR and 40% sales tax	Amount left for everything else
1	$50,000	$0	$8400	$41,600
2	$50,000	$0	$8400	$41,600
3	$50,000	$0	$8400	$41,600
4	$50,000	$0	$8400	$41,600
5	$50,000	$0	$8400	$41,600
TOTAL:	$250,000	$0	$42,000	$208,000

In the all sales tax model, your car costs you about $12,000 more overall, which doesn't sound ideal until you consider the offset from taxation that you actually saved $50,500 over the same time period, with the same interest rate, the same salary, and the same amortization schedule. Your wages, however, would likely increase because they would no longer be disincentivized. You would likely make up the $12,000 difference easily over the course of five years with increased wages. Businesses would likewise see a reduction in their tax burden with the elimination of payroll taxes and the simplification of the tax code. These cost savings could then be passed on to employees or to consumers.

The criticism to a model like this is often that you would end up being hurt more in short term purchases. Imagine how awful it would be to pay 40% more for groceries! Let's test that theory too. Let's say you spend $300 a week on groceries. At a 40% markup, you are now spending $420 on groceries every week. Over the course of the same five year time period, you spent an additional $31,200. That only consumes a fraction of what you saved in not paying income taxes. The difference is that you currently cannot choose to change how much you pay in income tax. You could theoretically spend less on groceries or shop more consciously. You can't cut coupons or cut corners to generate a lower income tax liability. A 40% markup is also an extreme example. Many experts on this subject believe that we could have a flat VAT tax of 23–30% and still bring in the same amount or more in revenue as we do now with all of our current taxation schemes combined.

This does disproportionately impact lower-wage earners and the unemployed. However, there is a progressive strategy designed to compensate people in this situation that is called a prebate. These would be government-issued checks sent monthly to households that would be adjusted in tandem with poverty level metrics and designed to offset the differential cost increases. The prebate could be implemented progressively with the poorest citizens receiving a higher amount, or it could be blind, where every citizen is conferred the same benefit regardless of wealth. Let this become the new pendulum on a new tax track that Democrats and Republicans can swing back and forth on.

If all taxes inherently disincentivize the activity they are levied upon, then what does a move to an all sales tax model disincentivize? The obvious answer is spending. This is perhaps not the worst problem to have. While a tax on income depresses wages, and a tax on property depresses property ownership, a sales tax increase of that magnitude might impact the shopping habits of most Americans. Many would argue that with our high levels of personal debt that frugality would actually be a positive advancement in our society. Though, I think the entirety of the problem would be offset by the reception of a prebate check, and also by the sizable increases in paychecks. A conscientious spender might cut back on their expenses or make a greater effort to save their earnings. If you met the average American, you would know that they would without hesitation continue to spend and spend heartily regardless. It is unlikely that this would have any negative impact on business sales in any way whatsoever.

Under our current structure, there is a great hostility about the ability of the wealthy to evade paying their fair share of taxes. Revelations in the 2020 election cycle that President Trump may have paid $0 in income-taxes did not sit well with many Americans. The wealthy can easily hide their income and easily offset their tax liability. They can employ expensive accountants to exploit every loophole in the system that the average American could never afford.

Another source of contention is the untaxed wages of undocumented immigrant labor. This generates a great deal of animosity with working-class Americans. The presumption often comes in the form of an antiquated slogan "illegals are a drain on our resources". This statement is often equated with racism, but that is a shallow understanding of the grievance they are attempting to convey by saying it. I would argue that it is even misunderstood by the people proclaiming this mantra. The disdain comes from the ability of undocumented immigrant labor to evade income taxation, along with a whole host of other labor laws, while still being able to utilize certain services. This allows them to undercut labor costs to obtain more employment opportunities than American workers who are required by law to be provided fair compensation. The concern that they have is that this is yet another group that is not paying its fair share of the tax liability, which is then shouldered entirely on the backs of the working middle class. As there is little they can do to complete the rich to pay their fair share, undocumented immigrants become an easy scapegoat.

Both of these problems become immediately remedied by the imposition of a sales tax. Now the undocumented immigrant, the blue-collar worker, and the extravagantly rich are all paying the same rate. The rich will inherently pay more by virtue of buying more expensive products. They cannot hire a fleet of accountants to get out of paying this one. The government would actually collect far more in revenue than it presently does off such an arrangement just because the wealthy would for once actually have to pay their taxes. It's much more difficult to hide sales than it is to hide wage earnings.

This is a golden opportunity for Democrats to assemble a winning coalition. It alleviates middle-class tax burdens, reduces the hostility against immigrants, and forces the rich to pay their fair share. It incentivizes wage growth and helps businesses. With the prebate it alleviates the potential harm caused to the poor. It's a win for everybody.

Killing Captain Crunch: The Path to Statehood and the End of Colonial Rule

- Immediately confer statehood to Washington D.C. and Puerto Rico.
- Voting Delegation in House for Guam, American Samoa, Virgin Isles, and Marianas.
- Reconsider Native American Statehood
- The Jefferson State Compromise

Puerto Rico

Approximately 3.194 million people live in Puerto Rico in the present day. If it were to become our 51st state, it would be the 31st in terms of population. Contrast this with our thirteen original colonies with a combined total population of approximately 2.5 million at the time of the Revolution and it seems more unconscionable that Puerto Ricans do not enjoy congressional representation.

As of November 3rd, 2020 Puerto Rico has voted in favor of statehood in an election that was widely attended. There is absolutely no legitimate governmental reason for the Senate to delay in taking up this motion. If we are truly a nation that values democracy and self-determination, it would be hypocritical to ignore or deny this request for statehood.

Republican Majority Leader Mitch McConnel has made it abundantly clear that he will obstruct any legislation brought forth towards Puerto Rican statehood on the basis that it would almost certainly permanently eliminate the ability of Republicans to obtain a Senate majority again in the future. This is something that I can fully support, as Republicans are entirely undeserving of controlling the Senate as they have proven to be completely incapable of governing for years now. If your only option to win is to suppress the representation of 3.2 million people, then you have lost the mandate to govern.

This would force the Republican coalition to undergo a paramount shift, which it desperately needs. While I am primarily complaining about the need of Democrats to recapture rural voters, it is equally important that Republicans begin to moderate themselves towards recapturing urban voters. The divisiveness is not just a one-sided coin. They are both destroying the country with partisanship.

Washington D.C.

Washington D.C. is similarly situated, though a tougher case for statehood. The population of nearly 700,000 is still greater than that of the states of Vermont and Wyoming. The difficulty with this argument goes back to the purpose of the founding of the District. Originally it was selected for its central location, the idea being that it would be neutral to the states. They opted to keep the District outside of the existing states because no state wanted to give that much leverage to a rival state.

If you read between the tea leaves, the entire Constitution is designed on the basis of a battle between urban and rural interests. Men of true democratic interests would have sensibly selected New York, Boston, or Philadelphia for the nation's capital, but their concerns are well documented. The Senate was meant to be a check on urban interests. The House was meant to be the democratic body. It has upheld this mandate well. There was also the egregious 3/5ths Compromise granting slave-owning states a greater vote count, but also diminishing their power in an attempt to keep their interests from being overbearing on the non-slaveholding states. That is how we ended up with the great swamp city for our federal bureaucracy.

Fast-forward to the year 2020 and frankly, this argument has reached the point of being untenable nonsense. At the drafting of the Constitution, the population of our largest colony was approximately 12 times larger than our smallest colony. In 2020 our largest state has a population that is 68 times larger than our smallest state. The idea that a state with a population size less than a small mid-sized city gets two senators, while a state with a population larger than most countries also only gets two centers is clearly a disgrace to democracy. That is not a check on urban interests, that is the tyranny of a rural minority no different than the aristocracy our Founding Fathers conspired against when they formed this nation.

Not to mention that D.C. is by no means a central neutral location anymore or else it would be located somewhere between Kansas and Nebraska. Now it just stands as another stain on democratic values by which 700,000 people lack representation. There is no continued justification for continuing the neutrality of the District as it is now well understood and integrated into law who has jurisdiction over federal property.

Congress has actually attempted to pass statehood for D.C., but again this has largely been on party lines with Democrats in favor. It should be of no surprise that once again Republicans would obstruct this attempt at statehood, as the District is overwhelmingly Democratic. Almost 90% or higher typically vote Democrat in elections. What should be a wake-up call to the American people is that those who are closest to the realm of the Federal Government and those who work directly for it tend to be overwhelmingly Democrat.

This argument of course does not sit well with rural voters because they have a general disdain for bureaucracy. As you might imagine, voters in majority rural states do not want to change the current dynamic, because they would lose tremendous power and leverage over federal matters. Eventually, Democrats and Republicans are going to have to rip off the band-aid and do the right thing. It will shake up the balance of power for a few election cycles. Small state voters will be upset. However, in the eyes of the world, the United States can reclaim its position as a free and democratic society.

To reiterate, if giving people their right to democratic governance and self-determination is the straw that breaks your party's back it is time to get a new party. I will present arguments later for how rural interests can still be protected even amidst these changes, but for now, I implore rural readers to take the moral high road and put themselves in the shoes of unrepresented citizens. All of the things that rural voters fear by relinquishing their control are the things that unrepresented voters actually experience on a daily basis.

Island Territories

This leads us to the remaining U.S. territorial possessions. Remnants of our brief stint with colonialism and spoils of war that are not quite within the realm of statehood yet, and may never reach that population size. The closest within range would be Guam and the Virgin Islands. There are also the Northern Mariana Islands and American Samoa which have very small populations relative to the states and their citizens are conferred subpar citizenship status.

It is not as clear cut what to do with these and there is a divergence of opinion among the citizens of these island nations on what goal they are working towards. The United Nations has been steadfast in pressing for greater independence and self-governance for Guam. The general consensus at the very least seems to suggest Guam would at the present time like to be conferred a commonwealth status.

There has been a suggestion of establishing a voting block to represent the interests of the island territories in the House of Representatives. This could be similar to how Washington D.C. is currently treated. It is at least a temporary solution to a complicated problem. Our relationship with these island nations, particularly in the Pacific is quite important from a perspective of national security. Chinese influence over the region threatens to undermine the U.S. position in the area and if the U.S. does not try harder to repair these relationships, we will eventually lose these territories to the Chinese. Increasing their representation in our government would likely go a long way towards maintaining these important assets.

In the interest of unity, I propose an alternative suggestion, which so far as I know, has not been considered. This may be in large part due to matters of cultural distinctiveness and the desire to maintain a certain degree of nationalistic independence among the islands, however, there is strength in numbers. If we assess the situation geographically, it stands to reason that the U.S. pacific assets could be annexed by the state of Hawaii. This would not disrupt the overall balance of power in the federal government, but it would certainly bolster the state's influence and provide representation to those smaller territories that cannot stand as states on their own accord. Similarly, the Virgin Islands could be annexed as part of a new state of Puerto Rico. Though the cultural divide between them is perhaps more pervasive, it at least provides an avenue for representation and resolves the problematic nature of U.S. colonialism.

Native American Statehood

There is perhaps no greater injustice in America than the treatment of indigenous populations. This is among the rural vote that Democrats desperately need to cultivate. It would be disingenuous to even proclaim that relations between the United States and Native American sovereignty had improved. The relationship remains vitriolic and both political parties are liable for heinous crimes against humanity.

The United States frequently ignores and violates its treaties with Native Americans. *McGirt v. Oklahoma*, a recent Supreme Court ruling has taken a major step in the right direction toward honoring the treaties of the past. The promise of genocidal maniac Andrew Jackson was that in exchange for the succession of native lands in the Trail of Tears, the displaced tribes would be granted permanent sovereignty over their reservation lands. This treaty was readily dismissed in the formation of the state of Oklahoma, which is rooted in thievery, malice, and racism.

In 1905 prior to the total dismemberment of Native autonomy, five nations met in conference to propose a new state. The Cherokee, Choctaw, Muscogee, Chickasaw, and Seminole tribes convened to draw up the State of Sequoyah, which encompasses what is now most of eastern Oklahoma. A vote was held with 86% voting in favor of statehood. The proposal was readily dismissed by Congress in an act of clear malice.

As we seek to heal from our past national legacy of genocide, systemic racism, and slavery, these proposals should be given greater consideration.

Over the past hundred years, the opinions may have changed on the matter of statehood, but the fact remains that there are presently no states which wholly respect the autonomy or representation of Native Americans. This has become readily apparent in the way in which treaties are readily disregarded and the will of the people is dismissed.

There is no greater example of the tyranny of the urban majority over the interest of rural citizens than the Keystone Pipeline project. Despite staunch opposition from Native Americans about the pipeline crossing through their tribal lands, the project was greenlighted. The use of eminent domain to ignore the will of indigenous people is a hallmark of U.S. and Native relations. The pipeline project is no different than the atrocities committed by the railroads as they plowed through Native lands. What is most awful about this situation is that the dismissed concerns about environmental hazards proved to be well justified as tens of thousands of gallons of oil have leaked out and contaminated the ground just as was predicted by protestors. An autonomous Native American state could have prevented this atrocity.

Due to the diasporic nature of Native Americans, the formation of a new state becomes geographically challenging, however, there are some prime candidates. Aside from the State of Sequoyah, the next prime candidate for statehood would be the Navajo Nation. With a population of over 332,000 and a contiguous land area of a size greater than many New England States, the Navajo Nation is well suited for statehood should they desire to obtain it.

It would serve the Democratic Party well to give greater consideration to the needs and desires of Native Americans, whether that be statehood or not. They make up a sizable voting block of rural voters throughout the United States and most recently delivered the State of Arizona for Joe Biden. Increasing Native representation is a small step towards righting centuries of wrongdoing, and it is a cause that I do not see on the Republican radar.

The State of Jefferson

It is not only the Democrats who experience representational disenfranchisement. There has been a growing and steady movement of citizens in northern California and southern Oregon who have made several attempts at forming a new state called Jefferson. The separatists were nearly successful in 1941, but the outbreak of World War II greatly stifled their movement. Subsequent attempts have taken on several names and attempted to include several different groupings of counties. It has yet to succeed at the ballot box, but the sentiments remain strong.

Voting trends would suggest that the State of Jefferson would be reliably Republican were it to be admitted. The total area of the proposed state encompasses about 3 million people, making it slightly less though somewhat on par with Puerto Rico. I only mention it at all because it seems like an obvious compromise. Both the Democrats and the Republicans could get a new "reliable" state, and the representation of the nation would be improved. While the people of Jefferson currently have congressional representation and it is by no means the same plight as those in Puerto Rico, it is an offering that might overcome the despicable opposition of Mitch McConnel.

Overall, I think it is important that we recognize the Constitution allows for and even encourages change and dynamism. Our relative stability over the past few decades has not made us stronger. It has not improved representation or healed divisions. It has not made for better legislation. The only thing it has made convenient is the stars on the flag and desks in the congressional chambers. As Americans, we should over the course of the next decade give great consideration to fairness and equity in representation. Our current system is wildly ineffective at this and change would do us good. State pride and cute shaped magnets might be kitsch, but democracy is more important. We need to redraw the boundaries of statehood because no reasonable system of government places the same degree of voting power on the half-million people of Wyoming as it does the thirty-nine million people of California. That is not an effective system of governance. Breaking up the larger states and consolidating the smaller states would lead to a more effective democracy and create less conflict in governance.

The late Democratic Party has boasted that it is the party of hope and change. It's time for the American people to see bold proclamations. Change the map.

Loving the Weeds of the Garden: Decriminalizing Marijuana

- Legalize marijuana at the national level.
- Immediately release all non-violent drug offenders from prison.
- Automatically expunge criminal records for these offenses.
- Tax and regulate marijuana.
- Reclassify other illegal drugs under FDA parameters.
- Redirect funds spent on drug prosecution into addiction treatment programs.

The war on drugs was a complete failure and there is perhaps no policy that enjoys broader bipartisan support than the legalization of marijuana. Over two-thirds of the U.S. population supports legalization. At the time of this writing, fifteen states have legalized recreational marijuana. Twenty-one states have legalized medicinal marijuana, but not recreational, and 11 more states have limited legalized use of medical marijuana. At this point, only three states have total prohibitions. It is despicable at this point that the Federal Government continues to prosecute people for this.

If you examine the current trends in states where legalization has occurred, it is estimated that legalization would generate 1.6 million American-based jobs nationwide. Most of them in the form of small business jobs. The resulting federal tax revenue would net approximately $130 billion alone. That is before taking into consideration the savings to be actualized from the $3.6 billion it currently costs taxpayers to fund enforcement of federal marijuana laws every year.

In states where decriminalization has occurred, we have not seen a reduction in law enforcement personnel, so the argument that the criminal justice system would lose jobs over this is untenable. It does, however, reduce the opportunity for unfortunate confrontations between citizens and law enforcement officers. It also frees up valuable resources that can go towards pursuing more serious crimes like theft or murder.

The idea of criminalizing the use of marijuana is in itself a violation of justice. This is a victimless crime. It only affects the user, and the degree to which it adversely affects the user is negligible. In any event, all avenues of modern research in addiction behavior, psychology, medicine, and criminal justice would suggest that drug abuse is best treated as a public health crisis, not a criminal one. Reasonable prohibitions on driving or operating heavy machinery under the influence are easily adapted or tailored to protect the public from the potential hazards of marijuana use from others. At this point, I can only surmise that its illegality is kept alive by propaganda from a bygone era and is a reflection of our geriatric Congress.

In the last 10 years alone, 8.2 Americans have been prosecuted for marijuana possession. This is outrageous. No other nation on Earth has the incarceration rate that we do. These prosecutions disproportionately affect racial minority groups. In fact, if you were to go back and ask the pioneers of the "War on Drugs" their sentiments are well documented. They couldn't criminalize race, so they targeted the activities being engaged in by minority groups. This is so well documented we find direct quotes and recordings of executive officials testifying to this. In essence, the prohibition of marijuana is a political crisis of unlawful imprisonment. As such, a blanket pardon should be issued. All of those who are incarcerated on nonviolent marijuana charges should be released from prison and all records should be automatically expunged.

Not only would this alleviate prison overcrowding nationwide, but it would also allow tens of millions of Americans access to employment opportunities and rights that were previously denied by their convictions. The economic and social benefits of this would be among the single greatest achievements of the century and would be a giant step forward for racial equality and justice. It is disgusting to have sitting U.S. Presidents confessing to the use of marijuana, while others sit in jail incarcerated for the same actions. This should be a source of shame for both Democrats and Republicans. Ultimately Democrats are the most poised to do it, they have passed it through the House and it should be made a top priority if they should happen to retake the Senate.

This is an issue that frequently affects rural communities as well. Drug use and abuse are not limited to cities. In fact, growing illegal drugs and producing illegal narcotics are some of the primary staples of small-town and rural economies. Let's bring this out in the open and freely enjoy the profits of vice. It is already happening anyway, we may as well benefit from it.

At this point, there are few Americans who do not know a drug dealer. I have known many over the years and I have known them to be outstanding people. They are not the gangbangers of propaganda myth. They are your neighbors. They are insurance adjusters, teachers, business owners, nurses, parents, etc.. Ordinary people who are just trying to make a living, who are being denied a perfectly legitimate economic activity. Let the American people have the freedom to choose whether to use or not to use. There is no reason why our current illegal drug selections cannot be adapted to meet FDA standards or those that apply to tobacco and alcohol sales.

Legalizing illegal drugs would also present a huge challenge for cartels. Those who presently occupy the fringe of society could come out into the open and compete with integrity on the market. Most of those who participate in cartel activity do so because they have few other legitimate economic alternatives. One of my favorite examples of a solution to this problem comes from the entertainer Killer Mike. His efforts in disenfranchised communities have been unparalleled.

He once helped bring together members of the Blood and Crip gangs in a competitive beverage enterprise. He offered them start-up loans, branding and marketing support, and business education. Legalizing marijuana can have the same effect. The need to kill someone or go to extraordinary lengths to sell drugs or smuggle them across the border becomes obsolete when you can genuinely enter the business without fear of prosecution. The war on drugs has only served to be a self-fulfilling prophecy through which it has created the very thing it sought to destroy. It is time for that to end.

It amazes me that a congressman could kick their feet up at their desk smoking tobacco and drinking whiskey, both of which are substantially more harmful to the human body than marijuana is, but then imprison someone for smoking it. The hypocrisy must end. There should be no further delays. The Democratic Party should make this a top legislative priority. If you want to win over disenfranchised rural voters, roll them a joint. I guarantee you will have their vote. The pearl-clutchers were never going to vote for them anyway.

Especially in My Backyard: Local Deregulation and Wealth Reconstruction

- Eliminate perpetuities in deed restrictions
- Ban mandatory parking minimums
- Remove highways from cities or bury them underground
- Disincentivize suburban growth
- Eliminate or reduce square footage minimums
- Remove land-use restrictions to allow for sustainable suburban and urban farming.
- Ban Homeowners Associations.
- Fund micro-projects instead of megaprojects.

Even as I write this book, every last space of grass is being plowed over in my community. The nearest street has three brand-new planned subdivisions being developed. In anticipation of growth, the nearby strip mall has expanded. Meanwhile, the sidewalk I take to walk to the park each day is cracked, overgrown, and falling off into a ditch. The creek is full of garbage. Other Strip malls sit vacant all over town. Empty anchor stores of a bygone era have stood abandoned for decades. Why do we keep building more when we cannot even use what we have?

When I purchased this home eight years ago, I bought it for $96,000. A similarly situated house in my neighborhood just sold for $205,000. The new homes they are building down the street start in the $340s. There are absolutely no jobs within walking distance or even a short commute of here that would support that home price. The Wal-Mart grocery store might pay $15 an hour with experience. You might make decent tips at the Little Caesars Pizza chain. However, as I drive around the endless expanse of suburbs I see absolutely no indication of a job market that would support a $340,000 home. The entire thing is premised on a concept known as "equity leveraging". You pay down your house just enough to qualify for the next tier. An interesting wealth-building strategy. Even a decade ago when I bought my house that might have been feasible. Where are the starter homes now? The average worker in our city cannot afford to buy one at these prices. Our city desperately needs affordable housing, but none is ever built. It's just simply not profitable enough for the developer. We never fix or repurpose anything, just build more and more future decay.

What's worse is that we know this entire model is destined for failure. The infrastructural maintenance costs greatly exceed the tax revenue generated by these suburban developments. Particularly when the state government caps out the city tax rates. The governor calls this "The Texas Miracle". Republicans grin ear to ear at their purported success. Look at all the growth and development they have created. The sprawl is so great you can see it from space. Mission accomplished! In a race to the bottom, they snatched up factories from the Midwest and brought them down here. Low wages, no worker protections, no taxes, hell in some cases we paid them to come here. It certainly has been profitable for many people. Yet we know that the profit is an illusion. It is only a matter of time before the bill comes due. The rich will move on and leave the rest of us holding the tab.

Texans like to scoff at places like Detroit or Buffalo. They equate it to the politics of liberals. The Democrats simply mismanaged their money and had too many taxes and regulations. "Texas is going to be different". The shiny new buildings have pulled the wool over their eyes. If you have traveled to the Midwest, it doesn't take a genius to realize that there is no difference in the design parameters of a place like Detroit and a city like Fort Worth. They have just recreated the same problems here. A few decades from now when those factories become dated and obsolete, they'll move elsewhere to the lowest bidder. The pillaging will start anew, and the people of that state will say the same thing. "Texas just mishandled its funds. We're going to do this differently". It is necessary that we realize, and realize it quickly, that our suburban car-oriented society is ultimately a failure.

Democrats claim to be the party of urban voters and that certainly seems to ring true at the ballot box. It is then Democrats' responsibility to bring an end to our experiment and restore cities to their former profitable form to rebuild the wealth of a nation from the ground up. This is going to take a grassroots approach at the local level and require some pretty significant changes, the likes of which we haven't seen in almost 70 years. Everyone expects change to happen from the national level, but what they really need is change in their own backyard. Democrats need to help their constituents understand that and offer guidance and support on how to do that.

Eliminate perpetuities in deed restrictions

Call me a huge fan of the common law rule against perpetuities. The idea behind this principle is that you cannot control the ownership of land from beyond the grave. At least not for very long, and with some exceptions. I would like to expand upon this concept and take it to the next level by going after deed restrictions.

Our system of deed restrictions and covenants on property has for all intents and purposes waved the rule against perpetuities by finding a loophole. It's not a specific person who is controlling the property use from beyond the grave, but rather the whole group of people who wrote that deed restriction. "I have dubbed thee oh neighborhood to be eternally suburban residential, and thus wave my magic wand of deed restrictions to bind this land eternally to that predisposition."

It's amazing to me. We recognize a degree of fluidity with individual ownership of chattels and property. I can transfer the title of my vehicle to someone else and they can either continue driving it or scrap it for parts. I can sell my chattels and I can rearrange them or repurpose them. I can sell you my property, or I can sell it to a group of people. If you are not making use of your property, I can, by way of a certain process, adversely possess the property from you. With intellectual property, we recognize a time and use limit on ownership. If I'm not using my trademark, I'm losing my trademark. My patents can expire. My copyrights can expire. This can happen to the living! Yet when it comes to deed restrictions, they follow real property like the Ghost of Christmas hell. Once it's been established, it becomes incredibly difficult if not impossible to remove.

In the not so distant past, people built spaces to serve their own purposes and needs, sometimes with limited regard to those around them. They established communities and built upon them as they became successful. If the spaces failed they were torn down and repurposed or they were given back to nature abandoned. Our current sprawl of planned neighborhoods and careful zoning has led to some pretty severe outcomes. They are not made to be changeable or adaptable. They are difficult to abandon. Reimagining a suburban neighborhood is nearly impossible without tearing it down, but the cost of doing so is equally prohibitive in most cases.

The deed restrictions are difficult to change and require a sizable congruence from residents, which often do not agree on how the changes should be made.

When we talk about the rule against perpetuities, we think of people as they are aged now. I could be 100 years old and give my property to my youngest great-grandchild under the pretense of a certain purpose, which could lock down the property for nearly two-hundred years. Back at common law when this was established, people were averaging out dead at 30. They knew even back then that land use needs changed quite frequently and that people of the present deserved to make the best use of it. However, they also wanted to respect the will and testament of the former owner to a certain degree. Then, of course, there wasn't the same enforcement that we had now. It's likely most perpetuities of the past could be easily ignored by the heirs of the deceased. Decrees and wills could be rewritten or misplaced with no means to prove otherwise. In 2020 deed restrictions live forever at the county records office. A suburban neighborhood appears to die on a thirty-year cycle, but can never be changed. We're being penalized by the mistakes of the dead and the living.

An easy fix to this would be to establish a law that led to the automatic expiration of deed restrictions after a certain period of time. At that point in time, the owners of the property must either agree to readopt the prior terms, draft new ones, or leave their space free for its best and most productive uses whatever they may be.

Unfortunately, this can be an uphill battle. Those who are successful in a dead neighborhood can easily continue to ruin it for everybody. We see this all the time in how they enact local policy, controlling every aspect of your property use city-wide. Then if you have the misfortune of living in an HOA community, you have an added dimension of overbearing neighbors. Eventually, they will all fail and will have no choice but to change their ways. The difficulty is getting Americans to understand why they will fail, when they will fail, and why it's best to pull the plug on them now before we hit rock bottom. Democrats at the local level need to start pulling the cord.

Remove highways from cities or bury them underground

If you cut off your arm, your body might survive, but your limb will surely die. As a result, you will have reduced functionality and periodically experience phantom limb pain. Most people wouldn't do this willingly. Typically it's the result of a terrible accident or injury of war. Yet when the automobile became a household item of the middle-class and highways were established, American cities were quick to grab the saw.

This may come as a surprise as it has been so long now, but everywhere in a major city where there is a highway, there was typically once a neighborhood. If we're being perfectly honest it was probably not the wealthiest of neighborhoods, and if history tells us anything, it was probably the homes of Black families that were demolished to make way for it. A typical pattern emerges. Wealth drains from the city. Neighborhoods severed off from the center of the city become stagnant and fall into an ever-increasing economic depression. Sometimes it gets brought back to life through gentrification, but rarely.

Despite all the fast-moving lanes, parking garages, and lots, traffic is still atrocious. I currently live only about 15 miles away from my job, yet it takes me well over an hour to get there in traffic. I have friends down in Austin who experience a daily two-hour commute one-way. In my experience, I don't even bother with the freeway. I take the backroads, which are actually six-lane boulevards and it still takes that long.

The city of Arlington prides itself on being the largest city in America without mass-transit. The irony of a city laid out end to end on a grid pattern is that it could easily and affordably run a highly successful series of cable car lines. Not that it would matter all that much. Few who live here work here. They commute to nearby even more urbanized areas like Dallas or Fort Worth. It is perhaps because our city has made the true construction of wealth impossible. Outside of the immediate university area, there's no part of the city that is walkable. Residents have little choice in how they provide for themselves. The road is king, and your car is your only lifeline.

This is not just a problem for urban areas, it is perhaps an even bigger problem for small-town communities. It's amazing if you think about it. In a city with one main street, where do you find the town's oldest homes? In a remote planned community an hour away? Not at all. You find them all within a few block radius. Anything beyond that became a farmhouse. The state of decline your smalltown finds itself in is now primarily related to its inside-out development scheme. The most valuable properties are the ones in the greatest state of decay and neglect.

Then of course heaven forbid that your town's Mainstreet got roped into a highway. It becomes a dueling source of nuisance and necessity. Motorists loathe the slow speed limits, but it keeps the town sheriff employed. The town becomes catered to the needs of the highway instead of the needs of the residents. Residents no longer want to walk there and it has little to offer them. They move further out to get away from the highway noise. Eventually, the town needs the highway to sustain itself and becomes dependent on it for survival. The town collapses when the highway is relocated to be closer to the residents who moved away.

For large urban areas, there are workable solutions to reparate this problem. Boston was perhaps the first to kick this off with its "Big Dig" project, which buried a stretch of I-93 in a tunnel that ran through downtown. It provides highway access to the city and serves as a main artery for vehicle traffic. On top of this tunnel rests an expanse of urban parks and plazas, opening up much-needed space for a little piece of nature and continuity to shine through. While the project was unbelievably expensive and poorly constructed, it opened up 300 acres of land within the urban core and spearheaded the development of Boston's Innovation District. Boston sewed back on the arm they cut off, and when they heal the wounds, the city will emerge stronger and healthier. It was a painfully slow process, but much was learned from it. We've seen many successful cities doing this in some form or fashion.

We must change the nature of how we view infrastructure projects. Instead of building new future problems, we need to focus on repairing the damage of the past. Reclaim the unity and symmetry of cities from the highways which severed them. We don't need more lanes, we need cities that function like cities were meant to.

If you ever have the opportunity to visit Europe you will see what a walkable design can do for the city. I was in London for New Years' around 2014. I had tickets to the Globe Theater of Shakespeare fame. I was supposed to meet a friend there, but I had fallen asleep and woke up late. I quickly traversed three blocks down to the Tube station. I jumped aboard the train and took it about six stops down. Just a few blocks more to the river, which I needed to cross to reach the theater on the other side. I hopped on a pedestrian bridge and walked across. I managed to make it on time. A process that would have taken me almost 2 hours or more by car, was done in about 15 minutes. That is because the city was built long before the invention of the car, and has been moving people by foot for centuries.

If you go to Florence in Italy, the statue of David is perhaps the least im-pressive thing amongst the massive pedestrian courtyards and the backdrop of the Duomo. One can walk for miles down the Mediterranean boardwalks of Barcelona without ever even noticing the passage of distance. People in these cities invested their energy and resources into creating timeless structures and designs that catered to the needs of people rather than the needs of cars. American cities would find themselves in a much greater position of wealth and stability if they started to return to this model.

The Interstate Highway System was developed with the best of intentions. It provided steady employment to the returning veterans of war. It sparked a thriving automobile industry. Perhaps the true motivations were not entirely about connectivity or ease of access. The United States had just invented a weapon with the capability of annihilating cities in one blast. It had just used this weapon to that end in Japan. The nuclear age had begun and it was only a short time before the Soviets had nukes of their own. As a matter of national security, the suburb was created as a means of defense against nuclear strikes. In its initial inception, the highway system seemed to be highly profitable and resulted in tremendous national growth. Unfortunately, no one was making projections about future maintenance costs and no one was considering how destructive this would be to the wealth of cities.

My great grandmother was a proud Republican. In my china cabinet, I have a special heirloom that belonged to her. It was a presidential teacup given to her by Dwight D. Eisenhower as part of his Whistle-stop Train Tour. It turns out that the president who would give us the Interstate Highway System, won over voters, traveling the nation by train. She and my great grandfather moved out to the first ring suburbs in Fort Worth and bought a small frame house. They would keep that house for the rest of their lives, even as the neighborhood around them completely collapsed and decayed into ruin.

Now I get to pass through this neighborhood each day on my way to work. I think about how one side of downtown thrived, while the other side collapsed. Then I recall how they relocated an entire freeway just to try to string it back together again. I think about the urban core and the wasted land space occupied by this blighted neighborhood that could have been a thriving metropolis. I think about the people who occupy these homes now and how they are denied access to economic opportunities and about the families stuck in an endless cycle of poverty. If only my great grandmother had read the tea leaves, Eisenhower's cup might not have tasted so sweet when she saw the end result.

Bury the inner-city highways. All of them. It's the only way to restore financial order to chaos. Consolidate the parking lots into parking garages. Then bury those underground too. Cities are meant to be lived in, not just traveled to on the weekends. We cannot just select the best skyscrapers for a niche purpose and turn the surrounding residences into parking lots. It's not sustainable. I cannot cut off all the branches of the tree and expect to keep its trunk alive. The city's most valuable taxable land sits under those cracked concrete lots and dilapidated first-ring suburban shacks, just waiting for reclamation and restoration. Repairing our nation's roads and bridges is a great election mantra, but let's make sure that what we're talking about is repairing the damage caused by our nation's roads and bridges first.

Fund micro-projects instead of megaprojects.

Vice Presidential candidate Sarah Palin gained notoriety for her purported conservative stance on sensible infrastructure spending, by claiming to have prevented "the Bridge to Nowhere" from being built. She alleged that she rejected federal funds earmarked for a proposed bridge connecting Gravina Island to Ketchikan while she was governor of Alaska. Like most Republican claims, it was primarily fictional. After previously supporting the project during her run for governor she then changed her tune for the convenience of her national bid. Although, for once she might not have been wrong if she had actually declined the funds.

The purpose of the bridge was to connect the city to its airport, located on the opposite side of the bay. A highway was constructed on both sides in anticipation of the bridge which slowly collected funds for years before finally being abandoned. Under a normal sensible system of economics, the bridge would only be built when the economic activity of the city had reached a point where it could support the bridge's construction. Rather than a "build it and they will come" approach, they would take a "build it because they need to" approach. Hence the expression "Rome wasn't built in a day".

Ketchikan is absolutely beautiful and certainly has enormous economic potential. It's probably one the best small towns that I've ever had the pleasure of visiting. While I arrived by boat, I'm sure the airport is a useful strategic economic asset to the community. It's a thriving metropolis of about 8,200 people. The initial cost just to build this bridge, much less maintain it, would have cost an estimated $398 million. If you did the math, that would equate to a one-time tax of $48,536 per resident and an unholy sum of future maintenance costs.

I'm sure you got out your wallet and wrote the mayor a check right? A citizen could ride the ferry across to the airport for approximately $7 if they brought their car. For the same price as the bridge, they could make about 7,000 trips across. If you were to cross every single day it would take you about twenty years to spend the same amount. The bridge was simply economic lunacy that has become a hallmark of large-scale federal projects.

For reasons unknown to me, there seems to be a pervasive need for grandiose federal projects that well exceed the economic potential of the places they get placed. I equate this to the federal coffers being like that of a newlywed couple opening their first joint bank account. There's something about seeing both of your incomes in there together that just presents the illusion that you have more money than you actually do.

Next thing you know, both spouses have dipped too far into the account and it becomes overdrawn. Normally, this would lead to an argument or conversation and the couple would come to a consensus on how to prevent such out of control spending in the future. That's partially because as citizens they are not allowed to run a deficit in their personal life. The Federal Government on the other hand is happy to spend well beyond their means because the deficit spending is of little consequence. Particularly when you're in so deep already. It's like the midlife crisis stage where you max out all of your credit cards because what's one more when you already have so many?

Ketchikan never intended to pay for the bridge itself, because when sensible people get together to solve their own problems in their own community, they would never opt to spend a fortune on a bridge that they can't afford and would bankrupt them. However, like all of America, they'll gladly take someone else's tax dollars and apply it to that cause. Who doesn't like to spend someone else's money? There's no fault or shame in trying, but that's terrible policy.

Imagine what else $398 million could be used for. What are the odds all 8,200 residents are using the airport regularly? What are the odds they are all of taxpaying age? We know the reality of this situation. It's even worse than $48,536 per person. In all likelihood, they would be better off if the government simply wrote each resident of Ketchikan a check for that amount and called it a day. At least they wouldn't have to find maintenance funding for a bridge they can't justify later down the road.

The average cost of a bachelor's degree from a public college is somewhere in the ballpark of $18,000 per year for a total cost of $72,000. For the cost of that bridge, the government could provide somewhere around 5,500 full-ride scholarships. One bridge, or 5,500 bachelor's degrees. What is a better deal? Well, it depends. If we're talking about the Bay Bridge in San Francisco or the Brooklyn Bridge, you could absolutely justify the bridge. That's because there is an economic justification for those bridges. Most bridges don't pull their own weight in costs and we need to start evaluating them with greater scrutiny.

I offer up yet another comparison. The average price of a single-family home in Akron, Ohio is approximately $110,000, which in my experience is actually way above the median there. For the same price as the $398 million bridge, the Federal Government could pay off the mortgages of approximately 3600 people in Akron. What would do more for the local and national economy? Alternatively, the average price of a single-family home in Los Angeles, California costs $650,000. That same $398 million could only pay off 600 families' mortgages. When we start to look at impact-to-dollar-spent, it becomes extremely obvious what we should be doing with federal projects.

You have three choices. A bridge to nowhere in a town whose residents almost certainly cannot afford to pay for it, 600 mortgages in an economically prosperous city in California that is probably contributing the bulk of that $398 million anyway, or pay off 3600 mortgages in an economically depressed region of the country. The Communists among us would do all three. Republicans would build the bridge and blame it on the Democrats. The Libertarians would have Los Angeles keep its own money. Those of us that seek to maximize value would realize that option three is the most beneficial choice for the nation. I'm not saying that these are the only trade-offs, it's just a dramatic example.

Democratic Senate candidate Barbara Bollier recently shocked the nation just by virtue of almost winning the State of Kansas. After polls showed her in a near deadlock with her opponent, the fundraising began pouring in and she had the most brilliant commentary to promote it. "Your money goes further in Kansas" I recall her saying. I certainly made my donation. Money always goes further in a place like Kansas, because there's not nearly as much of it to go around as there is anywhere else in America.

Democrats spend unbelievable sums of money trying to pick off a select group of House seats in places like Texas and North Carolina. Ultimately, there were no results to show for it in the 2020 election. Republicans are sitting safe and comfortable in a state like Kansas. Imagine how things might have gone if Democrats had backed Barbara at the beginning of her campaign the way they did in the end. Imagine the saturation of airtime that could be achieved in these ignored GOP strongholds. There is something beautiful about it. Campaigning against a Democrat is inherently more expensive. At present, the overwhelming majority of the base lives in cities. Expensive cities. Democrats have an absolute unseen advantage in maximizing the value of their fundraising dollars. For whatever reason, they just choose not to. There is no need to run campaigns in the cities when you already win them by 70% margins. Let Republicans shell out untold millions for city ads.

Democrats need to desperately reevaluate how projects are funded in this country as well as their campaign strategies. If we are truly the party of the people, the champion of the working man, the party of social change that is going to eliminate poverty and provide opportunity for all, then we need to start funding projects in a way that supports that. Make the federal dollars go further by investing in microscale projects. Instead of a bridge to nowhere, build bridges to prosperity. Make small scale improvements. A couple of tiny houses for the homeless here. Fix a broken sidewalk there. Restore an old commercial building to revitalize a neighborhood. Provide startup capital in places with no banks. I realize it's not as glamorous as saying you built the Senator Dickweasel Memorial Overpass, but at least you could say that you were being fiscally responsible. You acted with integrity towards the people's money and spent it on projects where it has the greatest benefit.

What kind of Democrat do you want to be? The legislator who added an additional lane to I-75, or the legislator who had the sense to use that same amount of money to restore economic prosperity to West Dayton? Listen to Barbara. Your money goes further in a place like Kansas. Spend wisely.

Making the best use of space and limited resources

One of the easiest ways to reclaim sensible urban development within your city is to target the regulations keeping the bad development in place. This is also the easiest to change, particularly because in general very few people pay any attention to their local elections. Local elections presently enjoy an abysmal turnout of about 15-25% on average, even though they tend to have long-lasting and severe impacts on our everyday lives. In my city, it's more like 2%! As fun as it is to squabble over who gets to sit in the Oval Office, who sits in City Hall is arguably far more important.

It is often the case that your local government becomes ransacked by developers, who have a vested interest in maximizing their own short-term profits by not only generating laws that are permissive to bad growth but actively force bad growth to occur. If you wanted to do the single greatest amount of good for your community you would run for City Council and be a bitch about it. Say no to everything. New fast-food-in-the-box? Better be attached to a walkable mixed-use residential complex. Pre-planned subdivision of luxury single-family homes? I'll keep the empty field thanks. The real estate thugs of your town will hate you, but your city will be taking steps towards financial solvency and good practices.

A target of interest that litters city codes throughout the country are mandatory parking minimums. The next time you fly into DFW airport, take a look at the ground below. Do you see a highly functional profitable center of urban activity, punctuated by a natural landscape of Blackland Prairies and productive agricultural lands sustaining the towns they surround? Nope. Not even a little bit. You see an endless concrete jungle with thousands of acres of empty parking lots. Many of the buildings they service sit abandoned for decades, only coming into play for a month out of the year when they become the temporary homes of Spirit Halloween stores. At least they found some use for those. If you think about how incredibly expensive it is to pour concrete and you think about how much useful space and natural space that takes up, you see that our current development patterns are the most wasteful, ignorant, and unprofitable in the history of the planet.

Home on the range was where the deer and the antelope once played, the buffalo roamed, and the cowboys drove their cattle to market. Man existed in harmony with the natural world around him. In 2020, even the squirrels are asking for rent controls because the space amongst the few trees that remain has made their survival nearly impossible. We have somehow labeled this progress. Next time you pass by the ancient archaeological ruins of a K-Mart, I want you to instead picture in your mind what it would have looked like had it never existed. Then consider how it might have looked if it had been developed into a timeless space of good use. Sometimes it is better to do nothing at all than to do something that ultimately sucks.

Consider where the most popular tourist destinations are in the country. When you are on the Las Vegas strip, how often are you disrupted by traffic patterns as you walk between casinos? How much money do you suppose is concentrated on a single street? How many interesting human-centered spaces do you encounter? Do you have to cross a parking lot? Did you have to use your car to go everywhere? What about while you were kicking back hurricanes in the French Quarter of New Orleans? Did you pass by any K-Marts? Does a stroll through Central Park in New York City resemble the half-acre afterthought park in your subdivision? Does your neighborhood have the same character and charm as a residential street in San Francisco? Perhaps you are not a big city person, I can certainly understand that. Was the local big box store the reason you went on vacation to Traverse City, Michigan? We know what good is when we see it. Your town doesn't have to have mountains, oceans, or rivers to not suck. It's all in how you use the space. Are you using it in a way that supports human life, comfort, productivity, and enjoyment?

Your town will love to make excuses for why it sucks. The typical reaction is that we cannot afford to build it. Somehow we can afford infrastructural maintenance on a new single-family subdivision of McMansions, but a whole street of shops sit empty on Mainstreet. It's amazing that cities in the Northeast have large conservatories and botanical gardens when their population is only one-third the size of our own, but we simply "can't afford it." We cannot afford any of the things that make life tranquil, but we can somehow always afford to eliminate business taxes to draw in a big box store. The city that could somehow afford to build two professional league stadiums within a decade, somehow can't afford buses to transport people to them. The reality is that it is all bullshit. Your town is constantly building things that it cannot afford, but none of them are things that make your city timeless or increase in value. They just turn a short-term profit for investors who are already plenty wealthy enough.

The second target for elimination goes hand-in-hand with parking minimums, and that is square footage minimums. These regulations started with good intentions when they were coming from the fire department or the public health department. We certainly don't want people exceeding the safe capacity of a structure and living in squalid conditions. That's not the kind of minimums I'm speaking out against.

My father purchased a five-acre lot near Athens, Texas with the intention of building a house on it. It's a small East Texas town. There's not just a whole lot happening out there, though many former residents have given it the unfortunate distinction of being the "meth capital of America". Would you care to guess what the square footage minimums were to build on that lot? Upwards of 3,000 square feet. If you want to put things into perspective an apartment in New York City of the same size (if it even existed at all) would cost upwards of $412 million. In Texas fortunately the price tag is closer to $425,000. That sounds much better until you take a look at the jobs available in the community. There is absolutely no indication of economic activity that would support an entire new rural subdivision of houses at that price point unless you really were making meth. It is no wonder that the developer went under and the subdivision failed to materialize. A delightful 1,400 square foot house could have been built at a reasonable price on the same lot, and he might have actually moved out there, along with the other buyers of the neighborhood. The subdivision might have thrived. You can easily fit a 3-2-2 with that size and achieve great resale value. The greed and stupidity of the developer, unfortunately, derailed the whole thing, costing what I imagine was a fortune to the city in unused infrastructure spending.

Millennials know all too well the devastating effects of square footage minimums. Most of us carry a small fortune in student loan debt. We've somehow managed to make absurdly unaffordable rent payments our entire adult lives. Now we can never seem to save up enough for a downpayment or reach a high enough salary to buy into the starter home. As a result, many have turned to communal living structures or embraced the Tiny-Home movement. Local governments, like online news media, love to shit all over these practices. Millennials ruin everything if you ask the city manager. The reality is that Millennials are actually trying to do the right thing. They're forging communities that are affordable, community-oriented, and productively resourced. The city code department can shove square footage minimums up their ass. This is the kind of development cities and towns of all sizes should be embracing. It should come as a basic human right that people should be allowed to a life that they can afford.

City developers only see the drain on infrastructure. "The tiny house community will overrun the schools!." "It will bring in the poor and the homeless" (as though they weren't already there?). "Public health and safety would be compromised!" "Where will they park all of their cars?" Nothing could be more ignorant. More units equal more opportunities for tax collection. When people are not burdened by their rent costs they can pay off their debt, save money, and ultimately spend their money. You almost hope they have nowhere to park their cars. When people have to walk to conduct business, guess where they spend their money? In your town. On businesses owned by people who also live in your town. A minor investment in a pop-up community of this nature can ultimately pay off huge dividends when those same residents become elevated. Structures need to be upgradable and flexible, so that people can actually grow wealth, instead of trying to amortize their way into it.

If your city code doesn't allow for tiny house communities or communes or other forms of "alternative" (even though it's actually more natural) living, then it needs to be changed. Democrats should make Republicans choke on their words with this one. For all the big talk about deregulation, watch their wigs flip when you actually agree with them. The reality is that Republicans have no interest in human-centered deregulation, and there is no greater way to showcase their hypocrisy than by saying you agree that there are too many regulations and asking them to do something about it.

The third target is perhaps the most insidious of all regulations, which are those that restrict land use and appearance. These are the real "nanny-state" regulations of America, that require approval for every insignificant change, force you to build a fence, and tell you what kind of grass you can have.

Some time ago, I looked into the possibility of getting chickens for my backyard. My backyard is by no means large by any stretch of the imagination, but to a chicken, it would be enormous. Naturally, there was an entire subsection of the city code regarding everything to do with backyard chickens. It went something like this; you could only have three chickens on a lot less than one acre, and absolutely no rooster. Then your coop must be of a certain size and height off the ground. All of which required some sort of permitting approval process. As you may be aware, chickens are grazing animals that require substantial vast acres of land to sustain themselves. If that sounds like bullshit, that's because it is. A handful of chickens can easily thrive in most suburban backyards. They don't require that much space. Then of course you can't get more chickens without a rooster, so that's not a very sustainable practice anyway.

I get it. Roosters can be annoying. They're aggressive. They crow loudly at certain times of the day. Chickens are in general messy. Then if you don't regulate them to some degree they can become a public health hazard. The reality is that roosters are only annoying because we are no longer used to living near them. The distance between our food is so great that we can't stand to live near it, and that's problematic because we have no idea where our food is really coming from. It's no wonder rural Americans are distrustful of urban voters. They would starve the country for the convenience of not having to listen to a rooster crow.

It should be easy to design a set of regulations that allows me to have a reasonable small farm operation on my suburban property without having to get permission from the government to do so. It's not hard to distinguish between that usage, and me starting a Tyson factory in my backyard. Usually, these regulations appear in the first place because someone tried to do it, they pissed off a neighbor, the neighbor complained to the city, and the city not wanting to ruffle the chicken feathers, thought they came up with a compromise. The problem is that this type of arbitration over the ordinary and productive use of land is counter to every facet of liberty upon which this nation is founded. The neighbor with the chickens is within their natural rights, and it is not the role of the government to rescue its citizens from minor inconveniences of their neighbors. Particularly, when their neighbors are trying to engage in self-sustaining timeless practices, and those practices cause no harm to neighbor's property. A sensible neighbor would grow a patch of grain and trade it with the neighbor for eggs. That's the basic premise of economics dating back to the beginning of human civilization.

The front lawns of suburbia are the greatest tragedy of the modern era. Cut green grass might look pretty, but it's useless. I can create the same ornamental effect with a front yard of lettuce. City codes that prohibit front-lawn farming are incredibly damaging. If I were allowed to do so, I would immediately tear out my grass and replace it with something edible. There's no reason to invest valuable freshwater resources on a useless plant. Grass is quite possibly the worst experiment in land-use in the history of human undertaking.

There is enough space within my suburban community to completely transform the space into a self-sustaining entity. We could grow enough crops and chickens to feed the whole community and have enough left over to sell to the adjacent neighborhood. We could install enough solar panels to power our homes. We could collect enough rainwater to sustain our water needs. We could create small scale commercial spaces and markets to trade and sell goods. In other words, we could make suburban neighborhoods into a more productive and profitable use of space, but we cannot do this currently because of the tyranny of over-regulation at the local level. Some of these restrictions might make sense in a place like Arizona where every drop of water counts. That provides a logical incentive to discourage lawn watering. If there is a sensible ecological reason to prohibit something in your community that's one thing, but in my neighborhood, as it is in many others, it is just bullshit appearances that are trying to be maintained.

The fourth thing that can be done about this problem locally is to eliminate Homeowners Associations. There's nothing I hate more and I'll refuse to live in a neighborhood that has one. After all the federal, state, and local prohibitions on the use of your property, why would you want to go the extra mile and have yet another administrative tier of control over your land use? It adds insult to injury and brings in additional costs that serve no purpose.

I once had a real estate client who purchased a home in what we'll call *Fakeass Oaks*, an overplanned gated community run by feral Karens. For the pleasure of this tyranny, the client was paying $250 additional dollars per month. When I asked about their overall satisfaction with the property after a matter of a few months, they told me exactly what they thought about it in so many unkind words. Fined for having trash-cans that weren't facing the right direction. Measuring the grass length with a ruler. Once the trash service had failed to pick up garbage on the street, and the residents received a letter chastising and threatening them for having the bags out too long, as though that were a force within their control. If you asked me to vote for a constitutional amendment banning HOAs, I would sign it in a heartbeat. The faster you ban these from your town, the better off it will be. Whoever invented them was surely not American. No one should have the right to exercise that level of control over your land.

Busty Burbs Federal Edition: Ending the Suburban Experiment, Rebuilding Local Wealth

- Establish HUD Suburban Buy-Back Program
- Revise criteria for HUD financing of high-density residential projects.
- Establish deregulated SEZs in America's most economically depressed cities.
- Implement Universal Basic Income, but call it something else.

Disincentivize suburban growth

While this is largely a matter of local deregulation, there are tools that the federal government can use to curb some of the bad practices while supporting the good. I've already mentioned the changes to the national highway infrastructure. The entity most able to control national development patterns particularly as it pertains to residential structures is the U.S. Department of Housing and Urban Development.

I feel that it should be worth mentioning the Republican strategy for this department was to put a neurosurgeon in charge of it because he was a major donor. The literal justification for his appointment to the position appeared to be that because he is Black, he might have a better understanding of issues related to public housing. This led to one of my favorite press conference gaffes of all time when Ben Carson told a wild story about how he had once attempted to stab someone, but the knife was blocked by their belt-buckle, in an effort to promote his street cred.

If that sounds ridiculous to you, that's because it was, and Democrats missed a golden opportunity to go after the incompetence of these administrative appointments. Cutting funding for an agency is one thing, but installing the wrong person for the job to purposefully run it into the ground is by far a new political low.

The Republicans of course would never eliminate the program entirely. The wealth of real estate moguls everywhere rests upon its lending arm. They just want to get rid of the parts that provide public housing for people in need. Needs they would never have if we implemented the previous advice I gave regarding local deregulation.

Current HUD policies are driving a large portion of this bad growth that I've been discussing. The loan programs are very popular. They have low down payments and good interest rates. Banks and lenders enjoy virtually risk-free mortgages. Flippers win big at foreclosure sales. Then there are large-scale residential investments that are a total cash cow for the wealthy developers. Unfortunately, HUD is just perpetuating a cycle of garbage development by enabling its continuation.

There are several unpopular recommendations, such as eliminating FHA backing for new subdivisions, but I would advise against those. Virtually everyone reading this who owns a home probably has at some point received an FHA loan to do so. Why wouldn't you? It's a great deal.

Just because a program is popular though, doesn't mean it's a good policy.

Current regulations do have some fail-safes. They require certain repairs and conditions to be met before they'll back a loan. This keeps them from reinvesting in already failed subdivisions. That sounds good in theory until you see the impact of that. Home prices in neighborhoods that cannot get FHA financing are rock bottom. Its residents are trapped there with no economic opportunity to escape. This tends to disproportionately affect minority communities and basically represents a revised and subtle form of Redlining. What are the alternatives then?

Establish HUD Suburban Buy-Back Program

Once a suburban neighborhood has been created we know that it's extremely difficult to end it or redevelop it. We know that it's cost-prohibitive to individual owners and a high risk for investors. In subdivisions that have reached a certain age and already failed, HUD could establish a targeted buyback program. If they're not going to back the homes for FHA buyers, then the least they can do is buy it off their hands

Land banks have been successfully doing something similar for years now. They buy up vacant properties and try to get them into the hands of the community to make better use of it. Properties that don't sell within a certain amount of time get put down and get sold as lots instead. A HUD buyback program could function in a similar way, and be substantially more resourced than local land banks.

Unfortunately, most of the homes that would be torn down in this process were essential to the community in that they provided low-cost housing that does not exist elsewhere. There are several strategies that accompany this process. One is to lower the availability of homes on the market using teardowns in order to boost the value of the better-maintained homes. The hope is that they will generate growth and reduce the social problems that accompany vacant properties. At best this model ends with gentrification where at least some of the residents are brought on board, however, this ultimately displaces another group of people who then become even worse off than they were when developers did nothing.

A better way is to be strategic about it. Contract for and buy up as much contiguous property in a dying neighborhood as possible. Then you repurpose the street or area all at once by redeveloping it. In an effort to avoid gentrification, HUD should coordinate with private developers to create mixed-use developments using time-tested financially solvent designs, but require that they set aside the same number of units torn down for use as low-income housing for HUD. In other words, HUD should be able to keep residents in the neighborhood that would otherwise be displaced from it. Not through a voucher program where they have to compensate the developer, but rather units that HUD retains. Not only do they retain it, but the private owners must be required to maintain it. This reduces the harmful impact of gentrification, it allows private businesses to still thrive, and it helps prevent future affordable housing crises by requiring a set aside for that purpose. Our current voucher system is far too friendly to the developer and the landlord. We already know that project housing has its own negative pitfalls. A hybrid solution provides a happy medium between public and private interests.

There are many projects like this out there in existence. HUD participates in some of them directly, but it should be expanded upon and more widely practiced. This works great for neighborhoods that touch the city. Those first ring suburbs can be pushed back into the urban realm because they are geographically close to it. Unfortunately, we're going to eventually have to answer for the exurban neighborhoods on the fringe.

The suburbs that are being built today are not going to be salvageable in the same way. They are simply too far away from the city center to be brought into a profitable fold. We could use the set-asides we're building within the city to relocate exurban residents when their communities collapse, but it's a tough sell. I would propose a redevelopment model from the field of biology. When a cell reaches an untenable size, it divides. When you get too far away from the nucleus, you grow a new nucleus. In these communities, it may be most beneficial to disconnect them from the original city center and orient them towards a new one within themselves.

Every exurban neighborhood is going to have an ideal place to do this. That road with six vacant big box stores is a prime candidate. Reclaim those spaces and develop them into productive spaces and work your way out. Ultimately you end up with an accidental twin city, but it's better than the alternative of letting every exurb in the nation fall into total ruin as we are doing currently. It's going to take some work, but if we can start generating policies that promote community, then we will see people start to solve problems like communities again.

Revise criteria for HUD financing of high-density residential projects.

During my law school experience, I had the opportunity to intern at the U.S. Department of Housing and Urban Development. Out of all the things that were not for me, this was quite possibly the most unsatisfactory. Almost weekly, the same group of wealthy businessmen would arrive in the conference room. Sometimes they would add one more, or take another one away. Each time they would come back under a different corporation name. It should be no surprise to anyone that these were all friends of the Governor, who were so extravagantly wealthy that they often arrived in the area by helicopter. These are not even my observations, but rather boastful statements from the men themselves.

They had found the magic formula to obtain HUD loan approvals for large scale high-density urban development projects. They would build apartment complex, after apartment complex, each one using the same approach and nearly the same layout. If you look around at any city in Texas, and at most "growing" cities in America you will see these endless sprawls of cookie-cutter apartment buildings. They're not much worth looking at. They don't inspire a sense of community. They cost more than most people can afford to rent. Many of them combine the worst of both worlds by being crowded and yet still unwalkable.

They would explain to me the calculations of the unit volume. In order to turn a profit the project needed only to be about one-third full. With all the comforts of corporate bankruptcy and government insurance on the loan, they were inoculated against all risk. They could just continue making and growing their money by snatching up a piece of land and building the same row of shit boxes on it without any repercussions. As long as they filled out the right forms.

The effects this has on the community are staggering. The average price of rent is so high that residents end up spending almost half or more of their monthly earnings on rent. Then in many cases, they must still afford the burden of upkeep and maintenance on a car. There is absolutely no benefit to the resident. They get a roof over their head, but not much else. Ultimately they are unable to save money and become stuck in an endless cycle of financial strain. They never get the chance to own property or to build wealth. The building they live in can never be converted or altered into something more practical or useful. The residents cannot transform the space for industrious or commercial use. There is really not even an incentive to maintain them. The owners have a calculated sales point as well. They know when these things become untenable and they have plans to abandon them before that ever becomes a problem.

All of it is temporary and serves the purpose of only generating wealth for the landlord. The landlord in this case has absolutely no vested interest in the community beyond his return on investment. The fact that this part of the city will one day look like an old Soviet Bloc neighborhood is meaningless to him. He bears no responsibility in the role he plays in destroying our society, because he will say "that's just capitalism" and that he did everything legally. Except that it's not capitalism is it? That wasn't his money to invest and that's a problem.

While this group of men was initially wealthy enough to at some point invest in the first complex, they had no trouble whatsoever obtaining government financing for the second, third, fourth, eighth, apartment complex. There was no risk of loss on their end. It's not capitalism. It's some deeply disturbed version of socialism, but instead of being for the good of the people, it's for the good of the aristocrats. Perhaps we should call it feudal socialism? All power to the kings?

In any event, this practice needs to end. Anything funded by HUD should confer an ownership interest to the occupants of the dwelling. The ownership of property is one of the most stable and traditional means of building and maintaining wealth. Perpetuitous apartments are downright mercantilist. They farm wealth from the inhabitants leaving them with nothing in return. To say that the privilege of living there is due consideration is a pompous analysis of the rights of human beings. It is in the best interest of the government to limit and discourage the construction of rental properties. Apartments should most often be purchased and sold, not rented.

It is almost by gross negligence that these projects are allowed to continue. As it stands these same six or seven men have probably well over 1,000 units between them. Each one acts as a leech sucking the wealth from its occupants. Imagine if instead, a group of 1,000 residents pulled together and constructed an apartment complex where each of them would own one unit. They likely would design it better with human and community interests in mind. The complex would be full instead of two-thirds empty. They would likely build it to last and be visually pleasing. Most importantly of all, when the loan was paid off, they could enjoy the fruits of their labor, by no longer having to pay rent, and by having a liquid asset.

Six men get rich making a row of shit boxes, or one-thousand citizens get rich making a community. The governmental interest should be clear as crystal. Republicans would likely defend this practice by saying there is nothing that would stop people from doing this currently. This is an argument that I find about as foolhardy as Mitt Romney's presidential campaign bid where he proclaimed that he knew hard times because he once had to sell some of his stock portfolio to get through college. That was a sob story best left in the Rolls Royce and right on par with the fictional narrative that the average worker has the ability to pull their nonexistent resources together to build an apartment megaplex. The theory of law in this instance does not align with the reality of society.

HUD should be there to help the average American. While it does this with single-family mortgages, it should also extend that assistance to collective action. It should not be a handout to the wealthy. It should come from within the community in which it is to be built. The requirements and regulations need to be amended and those amendments aren't going to be coming from Republicans.

Establish deregulated SEZs in America's most economically depressed cities

I hate to borrow an idea from the Chinese, but I'm at a loss for other words to describe it. "Special Economic Zones" are just a fancy name for places with fewer regulations. China started this journey in the late 1970s and it has been tremendously successful at attracting foreign investment and development. Chinese urbanism is perhaps a bit too similar to a dystopian sci-fi novel for my taste, but it's worth considering that while U.S. cities are primarily collapsing, China's *natural* cities are generally thriving. Particularly these more deregulated pseudo-independent ones.

Anyone who has visited Hong Kong and Macau or conducted business there has had this fantasy. Coming back to the United States you start to have visions about the seemingly steroidal capitalism that has driven development there. You wonder what we might accomplish if we took the same strip-down deregulation approach. I say it's worth trying in some places.

Let's take a handful of the most economically depressed cities in America. This doesn't have to be complicated. I could easily draw a map of where those cities are today and which ones it will be tomorrow. Gary, Indiana, Flint, Michigan, Youngstown, Ohio, etc. It is no secret that the economy of these towns is suffering. Valiant efforts are being made to try and salvage them the best they can and reinvent themselves, but you can imagine setbacks like the Great Recession and the Covid-19 Crisis can easily wipe out those gains. As we flounder with inaction, China continues to rise in economic power. The United States is struggling to maintain places like Cleveland, Ohio with a population of about two million, while China is somehow able to manage Tianjin with a population of twelve million. We cannot continue to half-ass hold a country together and reminisce about the glory days. It's not simply a matter of trade imbalances that are going to come back to haunt us.

Designate a handful of these struggling cities in the United States as "Special Economic Zones". Remove all the barriers and regulatory hurdles to running a business. Get rid of all those targeted local regulations we talked about earlier. Make it a tax-free zone. Then kick back and see what happens. Worst case scenario, it stays an economically depressed area and nothing has changed. I think that we might be pleasantly surprised by what we could accomplish. Once the city has built itself back up and stands on its own legs, you bring it back into the fold and then declare a new zone in the next economically depressed area.

The difficult part about this politically is that it's not going to have universal applicability. It's not going to be happening in every state or every city. There is some degree of jealousy involved. It's hard to get Senators and Representatives on board with something that only benefits one particular region of the country. That's precisely the problem with modern politics. The good of the nation must come first at the federal level. The fact is our chain is only as strong as its weakest link. The idea that a place like Gary could once again be a thriving economic powerhouse should be something every American wants. That is more money for them to spend in the economy, strengthening us all. We act as though success is poured from a pitcher where if I fill one person's glass there will be less for everyone else. That's not how economic prosperity works. It's multiplicitous. We can all do well and we can all grow because we are all doing well.

Implement Universal Basic Income, but call it something else.

Americans have been working themselves to death for decades. The pressure of constantly occupying our time with pursuits of labor permeates our society. Yet for all the blood, sweat, and tears they put into their occupations, millions of Americans have seen their jobs disappear. While we are on a course trajectory with the world's first trillionaire, the average American continues to see declines in every aspect of their net worth.

Housing costs more, food costs more, education costs more, transportation costs more. The needle on wages hovers on empty. More and more jobs get replaced by automated processes every day. Imagine in the 1940s it was necessary to employ entire warehouses full of letter transcribers. Each letter had to be hand-typed and hand-copied. Printing presses had to be physically set by mechanical processes. The invention of the copy machine quickly wiped out the transcription industry. Automation apologists will say that it created jobs elsewhere. Well, now we need manufacturers of the copier. We need copier maintenance staff. We need toner cartridges. Those do create some jobs. In the immediate inception of technology, the net jobs increase, but if you look ahead the technology becomes more efficient. It goes down in price. It becomes saturated into the market. Your former transcription warehouses full of women now have to find new labor. Only a handful of them will get to work for the copy machine maker.

It is not that we should stop this progress. There is perhaps nothing more absurd than maintaining a Toll Workers Union at this point in the century. I'm sure none of us are trying to make switchboard operators happen again or bring back video stores. Technological advancement is supposed to make our lives both better and easier. They are supposed to free us from the task of labor so that we can enjoy more time for leisure.

Instead what has happened is that technology has displaced labor without any systematic economic change, thus making labor cheaper, more competitive, and less available. In essence. the more progress we make, the deeper we dig our own occupational graves. Blue-collar workers were the first to get hit, but as artificial intelligence breakthroughs continue, our white-collar workers will soon experience their own mass occupational collapses. It's not a matter of if it will happen at this point, but rather when.

That is what makes it so depressing to see people genuinely believe a politician is going to bring their factory job back from overseas. Worse yet, they believe that if they just expel all the immigrants that purportedly stole their jobs, they'll come back again. Our government keeps telling people their goldfish ran away when they're the ones killing it. Your goldfish didn't run away. It's flushed and gone. The same is true for the jobs of yesteryear. Rather than making false promises that the jobs are going to come back, it would be best to acknowledge reality. We need new jobs that serve our modern economic needs, and we need considerations for how to best utilize our labor in a post-work economy.

Americans worked hard for the benefits of automation. The fact that they are not being compensated for their hard work and innovation over the decades is a violation of the social contract of our nation. A man does not become a trillionaire on the merits of his own labor. He does so through the theft of generations of wealth and labor from his fellow man. John Locke must be rolling in his grave over the abuse of Natural Law that comes with our national inequality. That money belongs to the American people, and it's time that they started taking it back.

Universal Basic Income is effectively a dividend on job-killing innovation. It is a celebration of American achievement and ingenuity. Every American, blind to their circumstances, gets the same check. As it stands now the nation's monetary earnings are being hoarded and held outside the economy by banks that I can only presume are run by dragons. Its effects are so pervasive we can see the economic drain visually across entire geographic areas.

Here is a hypothetical example. John develops a new piece of technology that affects a particular industry. There were 20 companies nationwide fulfilling that industry before. With the new technology, all of them have gone out of business leaving just John's technology upstart. He is able to hire the best people from the industry and discard the rest.

He employs 1,000 people in his hometown city of Boringsville. John and his friends Bill and Suzie make up the executive team. They decide to leave Boringsville to go start an executive office in Awesomeberg. Johns company brings in $100,000 a month with each employee generating $1,000 of the profit. John pays Bill and Suzie $20,000. It provides them a generous living wage and buys their complacency. John pays each employee $10 of that profit. He keeps the remaining $70,000 for himself. After all, where would they be if it were not for John's technology? Well as it turns out they would all be much better off.

Boringsville is generating $100,000 of profit, but $70,000 of it is getting shipped off to Awesomeberg. John's money is sitting in the Awesomeberg Bank. That's where he spends much of it. It's become so nice that even the sidewalks are paved with gold. One day John takes an elaborate golf vacation to Desperation City. They offer him a killer tax deal to move the company there. He closes the Boringsville plant, laying off all 100,000 people. He now pays 50,000 people in Desperation City to do the same amount of work with half the staff and half the pay as he now only pays them $5. The Boringsville economy goes into an unrecoverable downward spiral. John blames the whole thing on the Democrats. I could go on, but I think you can see where this scenario is going. It's a common narrative. Add quite a few more zeros to all the numbers to get closer to reality.

"Why is my community so poor? Where did all the jobs go? I worked my whole life. Why is my pension gone?" John wants you to believe the people in Desperation City took their jobs, but the truth is that John has been stealing their labor for decades. He screwed you over and now he's doing it to them too. It's all legal though. The people in Awesomeville are certainly celebrating. Yet it is still morally reprehensible. I call it lawful, but awful. Americans deserve better than that.

Universal basic income basically keeps paying the good folks of Boringsville the $10,000 they lost. John loses a grand total of $5,000 additional dollars of his $70,000 fortune. He's still a greedy sack of shit, but at least he isn't allowed to completely destroy a town using their own labor against them.

Americans are scared of Universal Basic Income. It sounds like socialism. It sounds like it's going to come out of their check. It sounds like a work of fiction. It sounds like it's going to add to the deficit. That's because they do not understand where the money is coming from, why they should be entitled to it, and how it benefits society. Democrats need to bring the message home. Money is multiplied in the hands of the many. Universal Basic Income goes straight into the hands of local people to spend in the local economy. In a place like Boringsville that $10 would go a long way. Awesomeville can't complain because they're getting the same amount even though they don't need it and are still pillaging their neighbors. That restoration of local money is essential to the revitalization efforts of a broken nation.

Andrew Yang was really on to something when he started calling it the "Freedom Dividend". It not only sounds better, it also offers a more accurate description of what it actually is. It's not a tax. It's the compensation owed for the price of labor rendered in the past that continues today. The main argument against this policy is the idea that people would stay home and stop working if they were given a check. The proposed amount of these checks are always so low that there is no conceivable scenario where the payoff is so great that someone would stop engaging in the workplace. It could however make all the difference in the world to that family and that community. It could also encourage innovative risk-taking that our economy desperately needs more of. When you're not constantly worried about being evicted or hungry, it's much easier to think about higher pursuits.

Fortunately, we no longer have to guess whether this is a good idea or not. A few weeks into the Covid-19 outbreak and even the Republicans were cutting "stimulus checks", another delightful name for Universal Basic Income. For many people that I know this check has been their lifeline. They've spent it on essential bills and food for their families. It has helped them across a very challenging financial threshold. This money in turn helped keep local businesses operating despite the reductions in sales. My wife and I used ours to get new tile in our master bath. Something we otherwise would not have done was it not for that. I expanded the wealth of my real estate asset, the tile company got some business, so their workers get paid. They surely did something with that money. That $1200 I spent, generated thousands of other dollars in economic activity elsewhere in my community. Ultimately, that purchase that otherwise would not have occurred probably kept someone off the scrolls of government welfare, and ultimately the government spent much less by giving us that check than it would have if they didn't.

Eventually, there will not be enough "jobs" left to do to keep our economy as it exists today in operation. If we do not start making the structural adjustments now, it's going to be a very rocky transition. Universal Basic Income today puts the infrastructure in place for our post-work economy. One where Americans can engage in labor tasks that they actually want to engage in, instead of what they have to.

The promise of a better tomorrow isn't typically that persuasive with the American electorate. They've been burned before. The people you need to win over to pass this policy have a few soft spots and I would recommend that Democrats play off their greatest fears.

In a capitalist society wealth inevitably funnels into the hands of the few at the expense of the many. The value of labor is essentially exploitative in nature with participants emerging either as "the haves" or "the have nots." When you introduce a robot into a system where people must work for a living to survive, you have made things more difficult for the humans. People competing against people is hard. People competing against robots is worse.

In a Communist society like China, the value of labor is predetermined according to need and ability. When you introduce a robot into a socialist system, it simply reduces the burdens of labor. If the robot is so valuable that it fully displaces your labor, your labor is reallocated to new needs and pursuits. Society overall receives the benefits, and whoever invented it probably gets a party promotion. The end goal is to have displaced so much of your labor, that you no longer have to engage in labor. In any event, the Communist laborer is not going to lose their house or their healthcare over it.

Their future utopian vision rides upon robots at work.

In other words, China only continues to benefit from the effects of automation, while the U.S. suffers all of its burdens. The technology we need to stay competitive is also harming our economic stability. Absent a significant change in the way that we do business, the Chinese economy will overtake our own. They already have a trade advantage. They have a substantially larger population and therefore a larger market size. They have landholdings all throughout the world. They control sizable amounts of global debt. Now we are seeing them flex their goodwill with countries the U.S. has neglected. We are seeing their military and technological advances steadily improving. We have also seen obvious disparities in the ability of their government to handle a crisis, versus our capacity to do so with the Covid-19 response.

Personally, I recognize that we are all human. I celebrate the idea that there could be peace on Earth and goodwill towards men. I want to see people healthy, happy, and prosperous in China as much as I want to see that here in the United States. The good of the planet and of our species transcends nationalism. However, I strongly believe in the pillars of American Democracy that all men are created equal and that they have certain inalienable rights including, but not limited to; life, liberty, and the pursuit of happiness. If we want to see these values propagated in the future, it is important for the United States to maintain its center of influence in the global economy. A position we are rapidly on the verge of losing.

If I were a Democratic congressman and I was trying to pass a UBI bill, I would market it with this approach in mind. Americans are highly nationalistic in general. There is nothing that the average American fears more than losing our global superiority. Decades of U.S. administrations were able to pass untold numbers of great, but challenging, legislation simply by reminding people that if we didn't do it, the Russians were going to do it first. We need universal basic income, or the Chinese will win. That's the big sell. If Republicans can use it as an excuse to give themselves a ludacris tax break, Democrats can use it to restore order to our impending inequality apocalypse. UBI keeps us free.

Doing for Country, While it's Doing for You: Expanding Service Opportunities

- Reestablish the Civilian Conservation Corps
- Increase funding for service-oriented government programs.

Having traveled extensively across our nation, I have encountered much of its breathtaking scenery and places of interest. We often overlook the historical markers that tell us about the creation of these attractions. There is one symbol in particular that I have come to look for. Usually, it takes the form of a long-forgotten placard, barely legible through the tarnished copper. The markings of the Civilian Conservation Corps show up in the most unsuspecting places.

Though it only existed for a span of about ten years from about 1933 up until the outbreak of World War II, the CCC has created a lasting legacy that we still enjoy today.

If you go to the Fort Worth zoo, there is an aviary enclosure, whereby you can enter and feed the birds. Prior to that, it was an alligator enclosure, which is why the current layout seems somewhat unusual for its present purpose. Embedded in the concrete you'll find the mark of the CCC. If you venture out to Caddo Lake there's a hiking trail that leads to a stone and wood pavilion bearing the CCC mark. Once you start to look for it, you will find it just about anywhere that nature can be enjoyed.

The concept behind the CCC was that it provided men with work in a time when there was little or none to be had. They were provided with some semblance of food, housing, and a small wage to send home. In exchange, they built roads and bridges. They built trails, they planted trees, they cleaned the roadsides. Many of our national parks were developed by CCC labor projects. Roosevelt's New Deal wasn't just about getting people back to work. It was about making America a better place to live. An alligator pen at the zoo is not necessarily a monumental government project, and it's certainly not a huge driver of economic development. It's just a small good deed, a microcosm of little improvements that brought up the whole system. What began as a collection of cages and concrete enclosures, has now evolved into one of the most successful and highly rated zoos in the world.

Current government programs seem to focus on large scale projects. Hundreds of millions of dollars for a highway overpass to keep the local construction company going. There's certainly a place for that, however like I have previously discussed, your money goes further on smaller projects and smaller projects usually end up with a greater net return on investment. We still have some of these small project programs, usually through specific departments almost like internships or governmental summer camps of sorts, as is the case for trail crews. It is not nearly as extensive or successful as the CCC. Case in point, after 20 years the sidewalk that runs from my house to our local park has crumbled into ruin and overgrown with grass. After 80 years, the zoo is still using that enclosure. Build things right, build things that are easy to maintain, and build things worth maintaining.

I envision a new CCC revamped for the needs of 2020. It would certainly include women and be racially integrated, an obvious improvement over its original implementation. There is no shortage of motivated young people out there waiting to seize the reigns of opportunity. Sidewalks need to be repaired, potholes filled, homes renovated. Turn them loose on the abandoned K-Mart and see how they can reclaim the space. We currently have many idle people and idle structures wasting space. It stands to reason that if we match the two together in a way that is meaningful and practical to the community that we could employ both to good use.

There are of course some great service programs already out there. Americorp is like the cousin of the CCC. There is also the Peace Corp promoting our interests abroad. There are more options out there than just military service. Let's expand upon those domestic service programs to build the things that make our towns pleasant to live in.

People who live in their community know what they need and what they want to see. They just sometimes need assistance with coordinating and financing those goals. A modern CCC would be able to transform those dreams into actions.

One particular summer I went with a group from my church down to Reynosa, Mexico. The church had a strong relationship with a Methodist school down there. Our church had just purchased a brand new playground, so we disassembled our old one and took it down there to donate it and install it at the school. There was no shortage of labor to be found, but supplies were limited. We ended up having to make several long trips back and forth across the border just to obtain the necessary hardware, concrete, and tools to complete the project.

While we were there we also visited a highly impoverished community for orphans and refugees near Monterrey. I had a profound conversation with a young girl about where she lived. She suffered from numerous health afflictions. Her home was made of three cinder block walls, covered by a tarp. The creek which ran by her community was filled by discarded garbage and toxic waste. Despite all of the great challenges with which she faced, she still managed to find joy, and use what little resources she had to create a life for herself. The will is there, the innovation is there. It is only the means with which to achieve it that are a challenge.

We also visited the grounds of the church community itself which sponsored the school. They had built everything from the ground up and they needed to create more housing to provide more opportunities. It was amazing what they were able to do using old and damaged tools, yet I knew that in my home community we would never have done things the way in which they were forced to do them by the circumstances of their surroundings.

A few years later, I was working towards my Eagle Scout rank. The most substantial component of achieving the highest rank is to orchestrate and execute a service project of beneficence to your community. Some of these projects are incredible accomplishments to be envied. Most of them are fairly modest; building some new park benches, installing a garden or planting trees, cleaning up a polluted park. They serve a great and practical purpose that benefit and uplift the community. I of course wanted to be different. In my community where I felt the needs of our neighbors were well served, I thought about how I could both help my community, but also make a lasting difference in other communities as well.

I ended up holding a tool drive. People could stop by our church and donate their used and old tools and building materials. These are things that usually sit around in garages taking up space. Eventually, they tend to end up in landfills. We would take the old and broken tools and repair and restore them as best we could. In the end, we ended up with two massive trailers filled with quality tools and building supplies. We took them down across the border into Reynosa, and we donated them to our church community there. Our neighbors got a clean garage, but our friends in Reynosa gained something much more valuable.

The trouble with most federal projects is that they can only see through a very wide macroscopic lens. They view the problem on its surface. They may conduct studies about it, but typically there is a process of guessing or determining what needs to be done or what needs to be made. Then the project is executed, but the problem somehow continues and it remains a mystery. What is to be done is already known by the people who are invested in the outcome. It is often not about what needs to be done, it is about the means to achieve it. All of the resources that we need are right here between our communities. When we start evaluating problems through the microcosm of human interactions, they become much easier to solve.

I have too much shit in my garage. You're trying to build a house with a broken pickaxe. I've got one you can have. I get my space back, your burden of labor is eased, we both get something out of it. Notice that I didn't go down there and build a row of fully completed homes. It was never asked of me and it was never the issue at hand. If I had taken that approach, the houses would fill up and when they went to construct the next one, they would be right back at square one. The nice row of big government projects looks impressive, but if it doesn't solve the problem it was needed for, then it has not achieved its purpose. I was able to fix this particular problem without spending much money, or investing all that much of my own physical labor. Sometimes the simple solutions are the best solutions.

For all the talk about "Making America Great Again," I have seen very little community action directed towards making it happen. Driving around and waving a flag isn't going to solve the complex problems of economic decline. Expanding our national domestic service agencies like the CCC would be a great step towards building our communities and bridging the divide between rural and urban interests. "This is what we have, what do you need?" Instead of "this is what you need, and this is what we're missing". We have much to offer each other if we only reach out and seek to understand the nature of our needs and the extent of our resources.

Curtail the Federal Department of Education: And the Horse it Rode in on!

- Restore local funding structures to schools
- Ban national curriculums
- No stipulations on school lunch funding
- Ban national accountability standards and testing
- Eliminate all student loan debt and never offer them again
- Make student loan debt dischargeable in bankruptcy
- Expand educational grant programs

Restore Local Funding to Schools

When you make audacious claims like "we should get rid of the Federal Department of Education" people give you crazed looks. You have either lost your mind or joined the Ron Paul Revolution. Not that there is much difference. It has recently become an easier sell in the era of Betsy DeVos. Is the agency so important to the success of America that you would be willing to risk having someone like her at the helm for 4 or 8 years? The Trump administration should give us all pause about the expansion of national government. Libertarians have some merit after all.

Let us first ask how schools are funded. In Texas, it is on a municipal basis. Our local taxes are assessed based on property value. Those local taxes are collected by the local tax assessor. Most people think that those taxes then go to their school district. That would make the most sense. However, the reality is that only a certain portion of it goes directly to their own district. The state intervenes and takes some of that money and redistributes it to rural school districts. This comes from our state constitutional requirements to fund schools equitably. It's been aptly dubbed the "Robinhood Act" because it takes from the wealthy districts and gives to the poor districts.

It was not the will of the legislature as much as it was by court proclamation that this bill was passed. It's come under many subsequent problems. In an effort to curtail the ever-increasing property taxes, the state has passed numerous bills aimed at curtailing the amount of taxes a local district can collect, even if the majority of voters in that district opted to raise them. The state's inability to constitutionally tax property has caused many of these bills to falter. Ultimately, Texas's efforts to circumvent all forms of taxation have created a slew of constitutional issues. If they do not raise taxes they run the risk of deficit which is also prohibited. However, if they raise taxes they also have to amend the Constitution to do that. If they did, Texas voters would probably throw them out of office. It's a real dilemma that is entirely unproductive.

Democrats have recently discovered that if they run campaigns around this issue of appropriate school finance, they can win in our more purple districts. A college buddy of mine, Jimmy Talarico, recently won reelection in the once Republican stronghold of Williamson County. Despite his opponent spending millions of dollars to try and unseat him, running a nasty and entirely unfounded slander campaign, Jimmy stayed positive and on message. He's proven to be somewhat of a firebrand in the statehouse of getting things passed across the aisle. His primary campaign message was education finance reform. That's what Democrats need to do to win Texas. Grassroots on the ground, and candidates that stay on message about the issues. Jimmy and I might disagree on how to fix the education financing debacle, but at least he's trying to do something about it for the good of our society.

Rural districts of course have profited tremendously from Robinhood. It was previously just a well-known fact of life that schools were not equitable. They were locally financed and operated. Your neighborhood built the schools that it could afford based on the economic activity that occurred in your school district. Hence the term "independent school district." That meant that there was a huge disparity in what schools might look like in places of concentrated wealth like Plano versus what schools might look like in a place like Joshua. At the time Robinhood came into being there was a notable performance gap between student groups. It should be no surprise to anyone that this could be seen primarily in rural districts and inner-city districts. This also meant that there was a sizable performance gap among racial demographics as well.

It wasn't a good look and the courts found it to be inequitable enough to intervene. The presumption that intervention is needed is problematic. Public schools are meant to serve the needs of their communities and historically take on the character of the community. When school districts were entirely financed locally, they were actually subject to greater accountability. If people in a rural district wanted better schools, they could raise their taxes to do that. If they wanted to implement a specific training program that was needed in their area they could do that. If they wanted to improve certain academic performance indices they could tailor their programs to address that. If something wasn't going right, the voters could easily change it.

That is the difference between the accountability of today and that of the past. We now have state standardized tests and a whole host of flaming hoops schools have to jump through just to gain access to their own money. This was accountability that we never needed. Elections were the accountability. If your district was being run poorly, you voted the school board out in the next election cycle.

It was also considerably more difficult to get away with nonsense. A group of angry parents and concerned citizens is much harder to ignore when you live next door to them. In our current framework, terrible administrators can throw up their hands and say everything was out of their control. It is all the state and Federal Government's fault. They wouldn't even be wrong. The will of the people is supplanted by the will of the state. A diverse and highly divergent state with very competitive and distinctive interests. Those impacted by the policy are less empowered to solve their own problems, and that is why problems persist and continue to get worse.

Here is a fantastic example happening right now. School districts in large urban areas understandably want to shut down during the Covid-19 Crisis in order to stop community spread. They have the technology and capacity to go fully online and they have the support of voters.

Under a normal, rational, democratic government Houston schools should be able to do that without having to go to the state for permission. Similarly, a district like say Motley County with all 150 of its students may have no need or desire to shutdown. They should be able to stay open. Unfortunately, under our current system, they have no choice but to beg the Texas Education Agency to bestow them the gift of autonomy. If Houston wants to shutdown it has to ask a handful of people in the governor's office to allow that, and then it has to get permission from Betsy Devos. Otherwise, it loses the funding necessary to remain operational.

It's hard to imagine any rational society adopting this policy. Houston is the fourth-largest city in the entire United States. If it were to break off and form its own independent nation it would rank 28th in global GDP. What hubris gives the remainder of the state of Texas dominion over the world's 28th largest GDP? If the tax assessor of Houston were to altogether stop remitting payments to the state, Texas would struggle to find the financial resources to even go after it. While the Supremacy Clause of our Constitution prevents such actions, there is also the unwritten common law of "No! We're not going to do that". It's the same rule by which the people of America realized it was stupid to be governed by an island across the ocean, and the subject of a delightful Twisted Sister album. If the local leadership of Texas' five largest cities came together and *told* the governor what they were going to do instead of *asking* him what they can do, he would surely have little choice but to capitulate. As much as we need structural order and hierarchy, we also need local leadership with a spine. Certain things are just best left to the locals. Restoring autonomy to local entities would go a long way towards achieving growth and stability.

At the beginning of this book, I talked about the concept of two Americas and the competing interests and needs of rural and urban voters. This is one of the most contentious issues between those populations. Rural districts feel oppressed by mandates that their economic activity cannot support.

Similarly, urban districts feel like they are being stifled and held back from being able to meet the needs that their city must address.

Instead of having a nice compromise where everyone is happy, we have a system where everyone is miserable and it doesn't work for anyone. It generates discord in the operations of the schools and puts them in conflict with parents and the community. This leads to a net distrust in the education system as a whole and undermines our ability to provide a necessary service. Ultimately, parents then opt to withdraw their children and their funding from the public sphere to put them in charter schools or private schools that are more reflective of their community.

The issue is that these two groups will never agree on what the universal formula for education is. In part because there isn't one, but also because their problems and needs are fundamentally different. When the state and federal government swoop in to try and come up with an overarching solution, they ultimately just make things worse for everyone. Restoring local funding and autonomy to school districts allows them to take the approach that they need.

There is no need to tip-toe around the issues like we don't know what they are. We know what is controversial in our communities. There is no reason why students in Houston can't have a comprehensive sex education program that discusses birth control and human sexuality, while simultaneously schools out in Granbury can teach abstinence-only. We certainly disagree with what the other has chosen to implement, but that ultimately doesn't matter. Neither one is paying for what the other is doing. Neither one is stopping the other from doing what is needed in their community.

Unfortunately, the state is quite fond of swooping in and undercutting the will of the local people. I recall a recent election where voters in Denton County chose to ban the practice of fracking, a measure which passed by a sizable majority of nearly 60%. A group of wealthy oil barons went down to Austin to bitch about it to the Governor and he quickly drew up legislation to undercut the vote.

This kind of underhanded anti-democratic bullshit is the reason we have such divisive politics. The people of Denton County have a vested interest in determining the type of economic activity they wish to allow. A reasonable electorate could reject the economic strain that comes with fracking and drilling. They could also reject the environmental stress placed upon them by those practices. They could also very conservatively say that they wanted to preserve their natural resources at this time for future needs or a rainy day.

There is a difference between denying someone a fundamental right to their existence and denying someone the convenience of engaging in a particular economic activity. This same distinction applies to schools as well and the differences in acceptable policies are obvious.

For example, no one is truly injured if Austin schools were to stop saying the Texas Pledge every day. Similarly, no one is injured if New Braunfels schools say the Texas Pledge once per class period. If that's what their community wants, it's not hurting anybody. However, if a school district in Texas were to say put all of their Black students in one class to maintain the purity of the races or ban Muslims from attending, that generates an entirely different set of Constitutional issues. In which case, the state and Federal Government would be rightfully intervening to prevent that from occurring.

Civil rights legislation is necessary to a free society because it protects the right of an individual's personhood. There is no such right to personhood for a hydraulic fracturing rig or to the Texas Pledge (though I wouldn't put it past our Supreme Court to declare it one!). Does the school district policy impact a person, place, thing, or idea? Reasonable people can understand why these are treated differently under the law. Before the state comes in to undercut the local schools, just remember School House Rock and "know your nouns".

No stipulations on school lunch funding

Continuing down the previous line of reasoning, but more applicable to federal funding, there is nothing quite as appalling as the hostage-taking of school lunch funding. This is how you know our system of government has entirely lost its humanity. Hopefully, we can all agree as a nation that kids have to eat at some point and that they tend to function best when they are not hungry.

Seeing as how not letting children starve to death is a fairly universal bipartisan value, I think it would be safe to go ahead and adopt a new education finance bill called the "Just Feed the Damn Kids, Asshole! Act of 2021". It sounds ridiculous, but in all seriousness, if the average American knew everything schools had to do for lunch money, they would be disgusted.

We know that child development experts universally agree that learning and life best function when your basic needs are being met. We have also developed a system by which children are dependent upon adults for their care. In other words, we as a society owe a fiduciary duty of care to keep American children alive to the best of our ability. This is not rocket science. Everyone can understand why we serve kids lunch in school.

Unfortunately, schools have to bend over backward to make that happen. They have to continuously meet federally mandated criteria and accountability metrics to gain access to that money. Our money. Money that we the taxpayers gave them to do this. This often means hiring an arsenal of unnecessary personnel whose only function serves to meet these requirements, which often have little bearing on the outcomes of student success. It stresses the systems and generates continuous frustration between everyone involved. If you were to calculate the amount received and compared it to the amount expended to keep it, it would almost be more beneficial to reject it entirely just to maintain greater autonomy over decision making.

School lunches should be integrated into the standard operating budget of every school and that's precisely how it should be funded. Imagine if the electric company told the school that after paying their bill, they would still cut the power off if the school didn't hire five additional people to implement and track a new program. We would think that was an absurd abuse of power and a shameful extortionist business practice. Why do we tolerate this behavior from the Federal Department of Education? Just feed the kids and grow the spine to pass a standalone bill for the ridiculous program implementations you want. The reason they don't is that they know that if they didn't hide it in the lunch bill, the American people would never support it.

Ban national curriculums, accountability, and standardized testing.

Education is understandably critical to resolving national unemployment. Prior to the Covid-19 Crisis, the United States was enjoying a record low unemployment, at least according to the metrics. Out of curiosity how many people felt great about it? Did it feel like unemployment was low and that the economy was doing great? Definitely not, because how we measure unemployment is a work of historical fiction.

Much like standardized tests, or GPD, or any other government metric, I can assign a set of values to anything and declare it meaningful. If I want people to think my education policy is working great, I lower the testing standards and then use it as evidence to support that claim. I can also raise the standards to an unreasonable level and then use it as a way to say teachers are failing at their jobs and only my policy can make them great again. We can measure increases and decreases on a continuum, but if it isn't real and it isn't meaningful, then it's useless. Most policies are useless.

I'll go ahead and throw the STAAR test under the bus for a moment. It is our state standardized test for Texas students. Parents hate it. Students hate it. Teachers hate it. Why does it continue to exist? Somewhere in the bureaucratic echelons, people were convinced that every aspect of life needed to function with industrial efficiency and needed constant improvement. It is as though the brains of children are going to somehow get larger and we'll be able to cram more knowledge in their heads if only we push them towards achievement on this exam. It seems that the leaders of industry are so comfortable reducing human beings to numbers, that they believe they can make anything and anyone into a homogenous sellable product. They are then shocked when the commodification of children is ineffective

I can train a rodent to navigate a maze and to push a button and release the cheese. If that's the goal I can get it to do that faster and with greater efficiency. I can increase the complexity of the task to a certain point. I'm considered a good teacher if I can do that. If I hand the rodent a book on calculus, it won't do shit, because it's developmentally inappropriate for a rodent and no reasonable person would ever expect it to do that. Yet the state will do things like that all the time when it comes to writing education policy.

When I was just getting the rat through the maze it was manageable and improvable. Now I'm a bad teacher because I couldn't teach the rat advanced mathematics. Asking me to force the rat to do something it shouldn't be able to do because it doesn't have the foundation or developmental capacity to do that, is standard fare for state and national curriculum designers. Anyone who disagrees with their ideas is branded a non-believer, no matter how well-founded their opposition is.

Did anyone ever stop to ask why we were doing this to the rodent? Is the maze essential to the rat's existence? Must it eat the cheese? What have I done for the rat by getting it to do this faster and more efficiently? The answer is harm. I have done harm because the mouse belongs in the barn, not a maze. I've just generated this social construct whereby I've imposed my vision of what the mouse should be doing and even though it's counter to the nature of the mouse, I'm going to make it do that anyway because I consider it progress. The life of the field mouse is very different from the life of the city mouse. Yet we put them in the same maze, which neither of them needs. Replace the rodent with a student, the maze as the school system, and cheese as a diploma.

It's impossible to design an effective comprehensive national curriculum and we shouldn't want one either. If everyone is learning the same thing, in the same way, to the same degree (i.e. standardized), then we're setting ourselves up for failure. Politicians try to project the needs of society in the future, but they are not fortune-tellers. Ultimately, uniformity leads to unemployment. If everyone knows the same thing and has the same skills they dramatically decrease in value. Then if everyone is learning the same thing, there will be no one to fill the jobs that require learning the thing that nobody knew. We're experiencing such gaps right now where we find ourselves having to import engineers and doctors because there just aren't enough to fill the demand.

America's children are stressed and they are miserable. We tell them which subjects are important, and then fault them for failing a test. There is nothing more depressing than watching a student who is exceptionally gifted in art call themselves a failure because they scored poorly on a state math exam.

Most policy centers around changing the way the tests operate. People will go to war over a passage in a textbook that always gets purchased, but never gets read. They'll ask for accommodations, extensions to deadlines, and changes to the content. This misses the point entirely. We spent thousands of years inhabiting this Earth without standardized testing. Now we cannot live without it? If standardized testing were to disappear tomorrow, would anyone notice it was gone?

The way politicians tend to frame this argument is that in the absence of accountability, teachers would stop doing their jobs. As you know, I became a teacher to put Caddyshack in the VCR and kick my feet up on my desk. We're all just chilling in the teachers' lounge hoping the test goes away so we can give up on the kids. That's the literal nonsense justification they use for keeping these tests alive. Teachers once held the same respect as other professionals in the community. In the absence of testing, we will continue teaching. The major disciplines will still be taught even if they are not emphasized by law. Our shortcomings will be checked by our principals, by our coworkers, by the parents, by the students, and the community at large.

In the absence of oppressive mandates, we could teach our students by meeting them where they are. We can prepare them for the needs of our communities. We can let kids be kids, enjoy their lives, and become productive well-adjusted members of society. Most importantly we would gain back valuable instruction time. I calculated it out once. The totality of test days and preparing to test days nets out to almost an entire year over the course of their K-12 education. That is not even including the time spent taking teacher-driven exams. If we cut out the government, kids would gain an entire additional year of instruction. Imagine the difference that would make.

Lawmakers like to ask how we would know the students are learning if we didn't test them. My response to that is how do people know you're competent at your job? Does your boss bring you an exam at the end of the year to gauge your performance? Teachers know what their students know and don't know. We know what they need help on. We often spend more time with them than their own families do. We know students are learning because we're human beings who interact with other human beings.

I can train my dog to select between four multiple-choice answers, and there's a statistical probability he will get nearly 25% of them correct, no matter what the content is. The state tests do nothing to measure real learning. Even worse than that, if you gave the same state exam to the legislator demanding it, they would probably score just as badly as my dog. The fact that Congress asks kids to do things that Congress itself cannot do is an insult to injury. Leave the teaching to the professionals and keep the government out of it.

I double-dog dare Democrats to do it. Throw away standardized tests, get rid of national and state accountability, get rid of national curriculums, and then sit back and watch. I guarantee the world isn't going to end, learning will still occur, and we'll ultimately be better off.

Colleges and Student Loans

The activities of the Federal Department of Education are of course not limited to K-12 education. They also play a massive part in our post-secondary education as well. It is perhaps in this arena where the most reform is needed.

We have determined that a college degree is almost essential for entry into the modern workforce. Then we have exponentially increased the price of attainment. Student loans are marketed as a solution. They have low interest rates and generous repayment options. For those of no other means, they seem like a great option. I certainly took out a sizable portion of them. Everyone who can do it should do it. At rates between 2-7%, you won't find a better deal on money.

The problem with this is that we need to ask ourselves why student loans even have an interest rate. If the government is offering you a service that it has deemed of such great importance, why are they charging you extra money for it? They treat it as though it were their money to lend to you, when in fact they are actually lending you your own money and then charging you interest on it. It makes sense if you are a bank, but when you're the government it's not even ethical. I recommend immediately suspending student loan interest rates and canceling any accumulated interest. The government should not be allowed to charge people for their own money without calling it what it truly is, a tax.

The second feature of student loans that irks me is that they are not dischargeable in bankruptcy. I often think of the people who were unable to complete their degree, or unable to pass their board exams. Basically, those who are unable to obtain employment to support that massive amount of student loan debt that they have. Maybe it was not the best use of the public's money to support them, but it's already happened, so here we are. We have decided to punish and compound their failure by making it impossible for them to ever repay the debt and denying them any relief. The reasoning behind this is that Congress fears that people would more often than not choose bankruptcy as means to default on their loans immediately upon graduating. I'm sure some people would, but it seems that Congress is ignorant when it comes to the financial habits of the average American. How many bankruptcies have you had in your lifetime? How often does that sound like a good option? Fewer than 1% of Americans file for bankruptcy in a given year. If allowing student loans to be discharged in bankruptcy is the slippery slope to a windfall of bankruptcies, it is only because the economy doesn't support the cost of the degree and we shouldn't be lending out that money in the first place.

That leads me to my next point. The economic activity of most places in America does not justify the outrageous cost of a college degree. The price that the market will bear for a bachelor's degree is significantly lower than the current value, because of the existence of student loans. It is not difficult to see how this happens. The majority of universities are state-funded institutions. Under normal market conditions, the state would regulate tuition costs to stay at a market rate that its citizens could afford. When the federal government is writing the checks, it disincentivizes fiscal restraint because it's a much larger pile of money. When you add tuition deregulation on top of it, you can expect it to continue increasing until they get cut off.

It's time for Democrats to pull out the scissors. We have out of control costs that have become all but a prerequisite for employment. We have several generations now saddled with massive piles of debt that they will never be able to afford to pay back. It's time to eliminate student loans. Forgive the existing debt and then stop issuing new loans. It's the single greatest thing congress can do for the economy at this point. Ultimately our student loan program that was promised to generate profit is on course to run massive deficits. There is no reason for it to continue. Statehouses can find their own way to regulate tuition and meet the educational needs of their communities.

As a matter of compromise, it seems almost certain that Republican lawmakers will never go for it unless they absolutely have to. One day they will. The economic realities of the program failure will eventually make that self-evident, whether they want to bury their head in the sand about it or not. In an effort to get that done today, I recommend a trade deal. Eliminate the entire Department of Education but bury the student loans along with it. Three generations can finally breathe, and Republicans can go home to their supporters and say they cut an entire agency from the federal bureaucracy. It's a political victory for all.

Personally, I would rather keep it but change its operating strategy. Those in academia reading this are probably quite upset with me at the moment because they rely on those tuition dollars and the loans they ride in on. That is why I recommend that we just expand upon the amounts and eligibility of existing grant programs. We can enable social advancement, keep our research institutions well funded, and not get stuck with an economy-killing debt problem. If we can have grants for projects and grants for research, we can have grants for people.

Higher education is still an excellent investment deal and critical to our success. We just need to be smarter about funding it. For all the discussion about how impossible it is, there's plenty of first-rate nations out there that have free college. It's entirely achievable. As universities are run by states, that funding would best come from the state level. Federal grants can help subsidize that mission, but the message comes better from the states. Imagine being from Nebraska and seeing what the federal government is issuing in loans for colleges in California. It's understandable why these states would be upset about it. They have no vested interest in that disproportionate payment system. Would it not be better to hear Pete Ricketts pass a bill that made Nebraska University free to Nebraskans? That's much easier to sell.

The hard argument against this idea is that states could be doing this now, but they don't. What will happen if that federal funding source is removed and states fail to act? The answer is that they dig their own grave. Let's say Iowa chooses not to do it. No federal funding, no state funding, no state regulation on tuition. Next door in Nebraska they're offering free tuition. You can drive for an hour to Ames and pay full price at Iowa State, or you can drive an hour the other direction to Lincoln and it's free. Which one are you going to choose? States that fail to act will lose residents and lose good-paying educated jobs.

The second argument is that some of the states that are economically disadvantaged won't be able to do this. My response to that is if we can't afford it at the state level, why have we been under the delusion that we could afford it at the federal level? It goes back to the newlywed bank account argument. That pile of money is not as large as it appears. When it's in your own account, you're much more frugal in how you manage it. Universities that are truly worth the value will retain their cost burdens. Universities that have been overinflated, will come back down to a market rate or close. Another possibility is that states can form regional arrangements to share the cost burdens, but I would argue that if your states have to do that to afford something, they might be better off merging into one state because clearly, their current statehood isn't that economically viable. Ultimately, I want to keep all of our universities open and growing, but states need to take responsibility for their out of control costs, or the nation as a whole will continue to lose the return on investment.

Another counterpoint is that we could just come up with a federal tuition regulation plan, but I promise you it would be a total disaster. There is no possible concordance on rate-setting between the states. It would ultimately advantage certain states greatly over others. Then it would be amended to where it ends up starving some institutions while overflowing others and we'll be back to the same system all over again. It's your state university, not the Federal Government's university. They have to be the ones to fix this.

I could write an entirely separate book on what good education policy looks like, but I'll save the rest for later.

Gored By Elephants: Improving Institutions of Democracy

- Abolish the Electoral College and replace it with direct presidential elections.
- Prohibit gubernatorial appointments.
- Nationwide Ranked-Choice Voting.
- Nationwide Independent Redistricting.

Abolish the electoral college and replace it with direct presidential elections.

The origins of the Electoral College are well documented. It's inherently anti-democratic by design. Its sole purpose is to represent the will of the people, while also protecting them from the tyranny of the masses (i.e. themselves). While James Madison and Alexander Hamilton spoke about it almost poetically in the Federalist Papers, what they really meant to say was that the American public was too stupid to vote and to protect them from their own ignorance, the electoral college would vote on their behalf just to make sure they got it right. This often gets framed as a defense against the city slicker coming in to dominate the farmer, but that's not what it was really about. Indeed it was quite the opposite.

The electoral college was meant to protect the interest of the educated wealthy landowners of the nation. A sizable portion of those whose interests were protected were slave-owning pieces of shit. It doesn't really matter what the Founder's intent was. We thank them for getting us here, but at the end of the day, most of them were horrible people by today's standards. We can and absolutely should fault them for that, while we're appreciating what it has led to. In any event, they are long since departed from this Earth and at some point, the living will be tasked with writing a better document. It has been a while since our last amendment, but we're due for several more.

While it was initially thought that the urban cities would overrun the farms if their power went unchecked, we now see that it has been precisely the opposite. Rural states hold a tremendous amount of power over urban states in the Senate. They have also been monumental obstructors of progress that are often desperately needed in those urban states. It is no secret why the wealthiest Americans have property in Wyoming, and it's not for their love of the outdoors. It's because their vote is the most powerful in the states with the smallest population. Putting it bluntly, it's cheaper to buy a Senator in Wyoming than it is in California. I previously spoke about the need to form new states to address some of the insanity of our unequal population distribution. That was only one piece of the equation.

We have discussed how difficult it is politically to form a new state. It's even more difficult to pass a Constitutional Amendment. There is however a genius solution to this problem that is currently circulating. The National Popular Vote Interstate Compact is an agreement between the states to select presidential electors on the basis of the winner of the popular vote.

We know that in order to be President, the candidate must obtain 270 electoral votes. The idea behind the compact is to gather enough states together that have enough electoral votes between them to reach that magic number. At present, the pact is up to approximately 196 electoral votes. It does not go into effect until they get all of the necessary votes.

It is imperative that Democrats push their states to enact this interstate pact. Here is the reasoning. We know that there is no possibility of obtaining the vote necessary to amend the Constitution. This is primarily because Democrats struggle to win the Electoral College even though they regularly win the popular vote. Let us look at the five times a candidate won the popular vote but lost in the electoral college. The first was Andrew Jackson who lost to John Quincy Adams back in the day when more than two candidates ended up with electoral votes. There was much more political brokering that occurred in the Electoral College at that time. Their inclinations were right in this case, Andrew Jackson would turn out to be a genocidal maniac when he finally did win the presidency. The other four times it happened to the Democrats. Samuel Tilden, Grover Cleveland, Al Gore, and Hillary Clinton. They all won the popular vote but lost the electoral votes. The latest of which felt particularly egregious as the votes of almost three million people were overridden.

Republicans know that they are losing the popular vote battle and they'll fight tooth and nail to maintain the electoral status quo. That is perhaps what is the most disappointing feature of this entire process. Rather than making the necessary changes and adaptations in the party platform to address the popular vote, they would rather hedge their bets on holding the Electoral College hostage. In essence, the Electoral College is stifling necessary political growth.

The argument that the popular vote would permanently railroad the interests of rural voters under the tyranny of the majority ignores centuries of what we know about political change. The Republican party of today would collapse in the Whitehouse if the Electoral College were eliminated, but it will not stay that way. New figures will emerge and take the party in a new direction until they find a new winning coalition. As fractured as the Democrats tent is, this wouldn't even be that difficult to achieve.

This is not about achieving a permanent Democratic presidency. This about the evolution of the Constitution towards a more direct form of democracy. One that respects the will of the people, because there is no longer a need to balance between the interests of rich slave-owning landlords and the masses of plebeians surrounding their plantations. Indeed we went to war over this under the Lincoln administration, and the interests of the people were victorious over the American aristocracy. Yet somehow, much as it did during the Reconstruction, these people just keep creeping back into American society and it becomes our imperative duty as defenders of liberty to fight them off again. Abolishing the Electoral College would be a sizable victory.

Prohibit gubernatorial appointments

While we are making our institutions of government more democratic, the next thing that cannot be ignored is the princely power bestowed upon the governors in the form of their ability to make appointments. This is a matter of state law and it needs to be reexamined. At the initial inception of the majority of states, technology and transportation were not all that expedient. It became necessary and a matter of great convenience for the governor to make appointments to positions within the bureaucracy. In 2020, that is no longer an issue. When a position becomes available it instantaneously shows up on the news. People know about it and can act immediately. It takes a while to put together an election, but it's not nearly as difficult as it used to be.

It is of course sensible that a governor can make a temporary appointment in the interim to fill a necessary position. The trouble is that these vacancies rarely occur by accident. They are often strategic and designed to prolong the governor's appointments as long as possible before the next election opportunity. Worse yet, many states have positions of great authority that are appointed by the governor, which should be reserved for the vote of the people.

The reasoning behind the Electoral College is very similar to the ideas driving gubernatorial appointments for non-elected positions. The governor is elected by the people or the people's representatives. Therefore it's still democratic as a conduit. As a democratically elected official, the governor will interpret the will of the people, by appointing all of his best friends to the judiciary to sanction whatever awful self-serving bill he wants to serve up that day. There is no reason why we should desire to give governors this much power and the fact that we do perhaps only goes to show that we are indeed too foolish to self-govern and that's what we get for it. The governor should be working for you, and so should everyone in his administration and judiciary, both as a whole unit and as individuals. Let's go ahead and make those changes to the state constitutions and demand direct elections for every position that matters.

Nationwide Independent Redistricting

As we are curbing the tyranny of governors, it is a great opportunity to bring up the topic of redistricting. The Census apportions the number of Representatives that the state receives. There is also local redistricting that occurs for statehouses. The districts are required to have an equal number of residents at least according to the time the Census was taken. There is of course very little instruction on how they should do this. This gave rise to the practice of Gerrymandering. This is where the redistricting commissions go through the state with a fine-toothed comb and draw out districts of unsightly shapes in order to secure their party's victory in as many districts as possible.

Due to the concentrated nature of Democrats in cities, it is often easy for Republicans to undercut their influence. Texas has adopted two strategies for this. The first is to create a district that absorbs a massive community of Democrats. My district for example typically votes about 90% Democratic, to the point that Republicans don't even field candidates here anymore. This gives us a reliably blue district, but it then allows Republicans to water down the rest of the Democrat vote using their second strategy. They circle a small portion of Democrats on the city's edge and then they draw out a wide horizontal district that engulfs huge portions of rural Republican areas, giving them multiple districts with guaranteed victories. It has actually become a source of amusement to witness how our out of control suburban sprawl has actually disrupted this strategy and I look forward to seeing what absurd shapes get forged as they try to add the five new equitably populated districts gained by our state in this year's Census. They might have won the battle for the power to redistrict, but they will still inevitably lose the war.

If our districts were drawn to make any sense where they might actually represent the needs of the people they serve, they would all be primarily purple. The parties are incapable of being impartial on this matter. Gerry-mandering allows them to save money on candidate fielding, and also leads to relative guarantees of coalition stability over a period of time. There is no incentive for them to stop. We need our Representatives to live in the purple for the good of the country. We need politicians who are always afraid of losing their seats. The competition is healthy for democracy. It encourages well-reasoned policy decisions that are favored by the majority because a slight miscalculation could send them packing. A Gerrymandered district offers no such benefits.

For the sake of our democracy and the restoration of reason in our political discourse, reclaiming the power to redistrict would be the single greatest step towards ending the lie of two Americas. An independent multi-partisan redistricting committee should be established in every state to oversee the process. They should solicit feedback from the stakeholders about the formation of districts. The goal is to have the correct number of districts with equal populations but shaped in a way that makes sense and makes representation an accurate reflection of who the people in their district really are.

Nationwide ranked-choice voting

It may come as a surprise to many Americans, but even in a democracy, there are a plethora of alternative ways to vote. Our current system of first-past-the-post inevitably devolves into a two-party system. When you only select one candidate, the risks of loss are too high to give consideration to more preferable coalitions. Your eggs are all in one basket and they either win or lose. Most Americans are completely unaware that there are alternatives out there.

Communism for example sought to avoid the pitfalls of two-party gridlock by enacting a single-party system. As there is only one party, the party will inevitably represent the interests of the majority, so there is almost no need for elections. After all, that is what Communism purports to be, the deliberative body of the people. That is the claim anyway. Unfortunately, single party systems are easy targets for the formation of dictatorships. The single-party inevitably begins to be shaped around the leader of the party, who purges their political opponents. As such, Communism is more likely to be just and successful when it's enacted as a microcosm by which participants are all directly involved in the decision making and free to leave to join in other groups that are independent of one another. Essentially in order to adopt a Communist model effectively, you have to completely dissolve the government. All of them really. People would form associations only with those who they wanted to. That's what makes it scary and confusing to people. It can be both dictatorial and nationalistic if executed one way, or it can be anarchist and community-oriented if executed another way. Therefore, it amazes me to hear so many Americans advocate for the dissolution of political parties. There are far more Communists among us than we thought, and they don't even know they're Communists!

How then do we fix a two-party system without getting rid of parties? One model that appears to have taken off in certain states experimenting with new voting models is called Ranked-Choice Voting. Instead of selecting just one candidate for the position, you rank the candidates according to your preference. If a candidate does not receive the majority on the first round, the lowest-scoring candidate is eliminated and that candidate's voters' second choices are then applied. That way you can experiment with your vote safely. Maybe I want to vote Green or Libertarian, but if they prove to be unviable as they usually do, I'll choose the Democrat. Maine seems to be enjoying it, and it has been instrumental in bringing new voices to the table there. Your state can do it, you just have to pass the bill. Presto! The two-party system is gone.

There are other ways. My personal favorite is the Party-list Proportional Representation model. You don't vote for the person, but rather the party itself. The party supplies a ranked list of its candidates and positions are filled in that order depending on the percentage of the vote received by the party itself. This reduces the possibility of populist candidates. Under normal circumstances, your fringe parties would never achieve representation, even in Ranked-Choice Voting. Certain voices are thus always silenced. Sometimes that's a good thing, sometimes it's not. With this system, you can still get representation even though you received only a fraction of the vote. There is usually a minimum threshold for how representatives are apportioned.

An example might go something like this; The Constitution Party gets 2% of the vote and it gets no representatives. The Republicans get 38% of the vote, they get three representatives. The Democrats get 20% of the vote they get two. The Socialists get 20% of the vote, they get two. The Libertarians get 10% and the Greens get 10% so they each get 1 representative. We've now managed to get multiple parties into office even though none of them obtained a majority. In order to govern, they must now form coalitions. If the Democrats, Socialists, and Greens caucus together they form a winning coalition of 5 representatives. These coalitions currently exist within our two parties, but they are required to form a unilateral platform. In the party-list system, cooperation between groups is required. If the Greens were strongly opposed to a proposed piece of legislation, they could pull their vote out of the coalition causing the vote to fail. Presently a defecting congressman in our system is penalized by the party whip for doing this. If they do it enough times, they lose their fundraising, they lose their committee positions, they lose the party backing. In the party-list system, the Greens representative loses nothing except perhaps allies they may need to pass their bills in the future. The Democrats and Socialists could still pass their bill through by enticing the Libertarian, forming a new coalition. The shuffling of the parties makes for better politicking because they can quickly overcome gridlock by realigning their alliances.

Another added bonus of this type of voting is the emergence of single-issue parties. For example, a group of individuals who are extremely passionate about marijuana can get together and form something like the Weed Party. They meet the voter threshold, they get a representative in office. They will then agree to form a coalition with the party that takes up their issue. An agreement that is easily revoked if the coalition reneges on its promise. There is no biding of time, the issue is addressed immediately or not at all.

There's more than one way to slice the cake of democracy, and I encourage Americans in their respective states to try something new. If you hate the two-party system, do something about it. Get a bill passed to vote differently.

Carving Mount Respect-more: Improving U.S. Indigenous Relations

- Honoring treaties and respecting Sovereignty.
- Expanding economic opportunities.

Honoring Treaties and Respecting Sovereignty

"A man's word is as good as his bond," or so Cervantes says. There was once a time in the very not so distant past where a handshake deal constituted a legitimate contract. Through the delocalization of economic matters and the expediency by which one can commit digital fraud, a man's word is only as good as your ability to continuously bother him until he performs.

If the United States ignores its treaty obligations and disregards the sovereignty of a free nation, then what good is our word? Moral reputation is important to our economic success abroad. In terms of getting things done, the world would sooner turn to China. If they want it done with quality, they turn to Europe. The United States sells itself on the value of our freedoms and our innovation. We have positioned ourselves as the moral police of the world for better or worse. Our moral interventions have a tendency to bite us in the ass later when we hand people guns and they turn them back toward us. Regardless of the implications of moral superiority as a sound policy, it's what we have to work with. Unfortunately, we have failed to look in the mirror.

While we are busy entangling ourselves in foreign wars and stopping the spread of Communism, the United States has been committing its own series of moral infractions. The Jones Act debilitates Puerto Rico's economic development and the nation is kept in almost a mercantilist state, being ransacked of its value in exchange for services it doesn't need from a motherland that doesn't support it. Our very Constitution was written by slave owners. We have seen the slow glacial progress towards racial equity, still to this day plagued by violence and incarceration. We're still the only country to actually use a nuclear bomb at war. Discrimination against the LGBT community is still rampant, after decades of violent repression. The land of the free has some serious self-reflection to do about how to make itself more functional toward the promotion of liberty and justice for all.

Our most egregious offense is perhaps our treatment of the sovereign indigenous nations of America. It's not something the average person thinks about, but despite all the efforts to exterminate Native Americans, they still exist. Their culture is often presented as though it is a thing of the past, what I like to call "Last of the Mohicans Syndrome", where they are nearing extinction. This may come as a surprise, but they are still here! They live in modern society just as you do. I myself am a card-carrying member of the Muscogee Nation.

My cousin lives on the reservation in Oklahoma. While he continues to learn the language and customs of the past, he was also an expert Dance Dance Revolution player. After working at Starbucks for years, he got a salaried position at an independent coffee roaster. When you think of *Indians* that's not what you see in your head. You've been programmed by a deliberate and ongoing propaganda campaign to imagine us living in a teepee or a wigwam down by a long-forgotten river. These past-tense visions erode the very real presence of current indigenous Americans and their needs. In many ways, it is that vision in itself that contributes to a self-reinforcing debasement. When people believe you are a ghost, what incentive do you have to try to be seen?

McGirt v. Oklahoma was a landmark Supreme Court decision rendered in 2020. It started as a longshot criminal appeal trial that centered around jurisdiction. In a surprise to everyone, the court sided with the Muscogee nation, granting them a substantial increase in control and autonomy over native lands in Eastern Oklahoma. This has significant implications across the Five Tribes. Senator Ted Cruz of Texas wrote; "Neil Gorsuch & the four liberal Justices just gave away half of Oklahoma, literally. Manhattan is next." Aside from the obvious vulgarity of including Neil Gorsuch in the pool of allegedly liberal justices, Cruz's comments are unfortunately misleading at best. The ruling is likely much more narrow in scope than what has been reported, but that's beside the heart of the matter. It was in fact never Oklahoma's land, to begin with. You cannot give away what is not yours to give.

The State of Oklahoma is built upon a legacy of theft, extortion, and genocide. The flagship University of Oklahoma even bears the mascot of land thieves, *the Sooners.* Colonial apologists would have you believe that Native Americas willingly ceded their lands in the east and migrated to Oklahoma, where they squandered their land and traded it for booze. As ridiculous as that sounds, it is, unfortunately, a widely held and reinforced myth.

This particular atrocity began in earnest around the time of the War of 1812. After White settlers encroached upon the hunting grounds of the Creeks, the nation fractured with many opting to back the British. It made no difference to Andrew Jackson who among them had supported the United States and who had opposed it. The end result was that the Creeks ceded over 23 million acres of land in a single treaty. Between 1733 and 1866 they signed no less than twenty treaties, usually resulting in a loss of land.

A contract under duress is inherently invalid. The definition of a treaty suggests that agreement is required. In this situation, the Creeks were given little choice in the matter, and whatever treaty was signed was typically ignored by the United States regardless. The Indian Removal Act was written as an authorization to negotiate the sale of native lands east of the Mississippi River. However, it's true purpose is stated in the name. They were forcibly evicted in what became known as the Trail of Tears, an act of genocide that indigenous populations of the Southeast have yet to recover from.

Most folk's knowledge of Native Americans ends there. The Natives were all snugly tucked into reservations where the remnants of their tribe weave baskets, fashion pottery, and open casinos. Come visit and they'll dance for you. That's the poisonous narrative afflicting current Native people. It is somehow comforting to believe that all of these human rights abuses occurred over one-hundred years ago. Unfortunately, the story doesn't end there.

For almost 150 years after removal, Native American's were subjected to government-sanctioned reeducation and assimilation programs. Children would be forcibly removed from the homes of caring and capable parents and placed in horrifically abusive boarding schools. Generations of Native American children were denied their names, language, culture, and religion. They were savagely beaten and often raped in these schools which had little if any oversight. This practice was not curtailed until the Indian Child Welfare Act in 1978. That means many of you reading this book were alive at the time this was occurring (and it may still be to some degree). Three generations of my family currently living were born before that time. These are not distant wrongs of the past. Generations of the living are still harmed by this practice.

This had such a profound and devastating effect on Native American families. My great grandmother grew up on the reservation. Her experiences were so negative that she refused to talk about her heritage. She burned her papers and did everything in her power to appear and act as a White woman. Not only did she not want to be outed as an indigenous woman, but she also did not want her children or grandchildren to know that they were either.

The real victory of *McGirt v. Oklahoma* was that the Supreme Court finally sided with the Native American position on a judicial issue. However narrow the holding may be, the fact that the case was acknowledged by the courts and rendered in their favor is what makes this case so notable.

It is such a rare occasion that it merits excitement and that is what makes it so depressing.

Native Americans represent a sizable minority in many rural states traditionally carried by Republicans. They are understandably distrustful of the federal government. They are tired of seeing their treaties and sovereignty violated. They are tired of being ignored by the courts. They are tired of being subjected to abuse and discrimination. They are tired of being discussed in the past tense. They are tired of being kept from economic opportunity.

As the recent Democratic victory in Arizona should indicate, the Native American vote can be highly influential. At the time of this writing, there were five Native Americans in Congress, three of them Democrat and three of them Republican (Elizabeth Warren not included). This is a divided electorate, but it does not have to be. Democrats have a real opportunity to solidify their support among the community, but they are going to have to take considerable action steps towards earning it.

This does not mean that they have to hand out reparations or kick all the White people out of their lands. Native American demands are not unreasonable. The first and most obvious thing to do is to leave them alone. Respect the jurisdiction of the tribe to self-govern. Honor the latest treaties and renegotiate those that are untenable. That means when a tribe wants to open a casino in Texas, you don't stand in the way. If the last treaty says that a piece of federal land belongs to a particular tribe, you cede custody of it to the best of your ability. Most importantly of all, when you want to build an oil pipeline, suck water out of a reservoir, impose blanket hunting restrictions over rangelands, deforest an area, build a wall through a graveyard, or strip mine a mountain to carve faces into it, you will seek out broad support from the tribal community, its leaders, and its representatives before you proceed.

This means that you must dispense with the practice of imminent domain on tribal lands. If it is truly imminent, the tribal council will work in conjunction with the state or Federal Government for that purpose. Otherwise, the government is just doing it because they can and it's easier to get away with if you do it to tribal lands, which is not only alienating to potential voters but also morally reprehensible.

Economic Opportunity

My second recommendation is to broaden your horizons on economic opportunity to extend beyond the walls of the reservation. Most federal economic opportunity programs center around those living on reservations. There is very little support for the diaspora of Native Americans who have left the reservation or never lived there in the first place. Their struggles are just as real as those who reside there and they have long been ignored.

This is not to discredit the work that the Dept. of the Interior is doing, but rather to expand upon its obvious limitations. Many of the jobs directed at improving economic opportunities for Native Americans pay low wages relative to other federal positions. This might be to maximize the prospective employment opportunities in economically depressed areas of the reservations, but it is making little progress towards viability.

Envision this for a moment. Your entire civilization has been uprooted and forcibly relocated multiple times. Millions die from a pandemic of new diseases. For ten thousand years your ancestors sustained themselves off the land, which is no longer an option for you. Millions more die in wars. The government has slaughtered your food supply to the point of near extinction just to try and get rid of you. The government steals your children from their home and sends them to reeducation encampments where they are tortured and forced to assimilate into a culture that is foreign to them. You can no longer communicate with them in the language of your people. Your graves are desecrated to build roads and buildings that your people can't even benefit from. You are forced to adopt a completely foreign economic system of which you have no capital and little understanding. Now the same people who did this to you want to know what they can do to help alleviate your poverty and suffering. The government put in a tax break program to build a fast-food restaurant on your reservation and hired three of your relatives at minimum wage. They then have the audacity to go into this community and ask for their vote? They better have a powerful message and an even stronger delivery.

I was recently in North Dakota where I visited the Knife River Indian Village. I encountered a Native American elder there who had come in from Montana to give a lecture on his tribal language. We talked for a while in the parking lot. He told me the story of how his people were screwed over when the Federal Government built a dam that flooded their lands. I was not the least bit surprised. I asked him what other sites of interest I should visit while I was in the area. Expecting some profound bit of sagely elder wisdom, he advised me to try the coffee at Tim Hortons.

Native Americans are trying to restore their culture and traditions, while simultaneously acknowledging that they live in the world as it is today. They are not frozen in time. They change, adapt, and grow. Some days you're restoring your native language, other days you're sipping a latte at Tim Hortons.

The Democratic Party needs to have an honest conversation with Native Americans, where the party listens to what is needed instead of telling them what they need. Recognize that the interests of individual tribes will be highly variable. Know that while there is great interest in relics of the past, there are also needs in the present and desires for the future.

Joe Biden's appointment of Deb Haaland to be Secretary of the Interior was a great first step, and I hope to see future progress made by this administration and those in the future.

Better Red Than Dead: Reasonable Socialized Healthcare

- Consolidate all national healthcare programs and plans into a single-payer system that provides a minimum standard of care.
- Regulate drug prices more efficiently.
- Fund healthcare research as aggressively as we fund missiles.
- Strengthen the CDC and its governmental affiliates.

Single-Payer Healthcare System

Democrats inherited a supermajority in 2008. They could have passed anything they wanted without consulting a single Republican. It became extremely obvious that the electorate was going to swing that direction after George W. Bush left office. There was a great deal of optimism about progressive and necessary reform.

It became clear that Democratic leaders in Congress were not prepared for it. Obama tried the best he could with executive orders. Instead of ushering in a new era, congressional Democrats spent the bulk of that time rebranding Mitt Romney's healthcare plan and arguing about it to death until we got "Obamacare". It is no wonder they lost so badly in 2010. They got a once in a century political break and they wasted it.

There were some great things that came out of the Affordable Care Act. Affordable coverage was not one of them. Amidst a crippling recession, it allowed Americans in their early 20s to stay on their parents' coverage. It provided coverage for people with preexisting conditions that otherwise could not get covered. It provided new coverage to millions of Americans. Those are all great results, but the means to achieve them make no sense.

I took a major entrepreneurial risk to start a company. My business partner and I had quit our jobs and gone all-in on getting this off the ground. Trump had promised he was going to make everything great again after all! Oil was going to flow, and regulations were going to be cut. Business was going to thrive. I never believed that, but part of me was optimistic anyway. It turns out my initial skepticism was valid, Trump meant Fortune 500 companies were going to thrive, and everyone else could eat shit.

Here I am in the desert with a new business and no health insurance. As we start to go about the process of hiring employees I realize that we had nothing of value in compensation to offer. We had the contracts lined up and tons of work to fill at a great pay rate, but that was it. Larger established companies had the same thing but they could also provide insurance, pensions, signing bonuses, retirement plans, nicer trucks, phone allowances, and a whole range of benefits my start-up operation could never dream of affording.

I turned to ACA thinking that it would be our saving grace. Maybe, just maybe, we could get a plan for the company that we could afford. After all, that was the promise, affordability. I investigated our marketplace options, only to be incredibly disappointed. Despite the fact that our profit margins were skin tight and there was only a handful of us in the company, it would have cost us thousands of dollars that we didn't have. In terms of insurance costs, it was actually the worst option available. We all ended up buying private catastrophe-only plans.

We're not the only company with this problem, and it's no surprise to me why Republicans are eager to repeal it. The costs of coverage just continue to escalate out of control. Families that were struggling already who couldn't get coverage at work, or owned a small business, couldn't afford an ACA plan and they were also getting slammed with tax penalties for not having it. If that was how the government assists people, I can understand why no one wants it to continue. When you start to really look at it, the purpose of

ACA seems more about keeping good jobs in the insurance industry during a recession, and I understand that. I would rather we create jobs that we actually needed instead of bureaucratic ones that fill space.

It's by no means the only healthcare program overseen by the Federal Government. We have healthcare programs for veterans. We have healthcare programs for seniors. We have healthcare programs for children. We have healthcare programs for the disabled. We even have an incredibly audacious healthcare plan just for Congress itself. If you total it all together, there's no government healthcare for the average working adult. If your job doesn't cover it, you have few options. If you lose your job, you might get COBRA, but that's temporary and it's going to cost you.

In essence, there is no government healthcare plan at all. We have a state by state, county by county public health network, but it's clearly ineffective. Healthcare costs are completely out of control and we have discovered our newfound vulnerability for pandemics. In fact, we have had one of the worst if not *the worst* response to the COVID-19 crisis. As much fun as it would be to blame the entirety of the crisis on Trump's Presidency, it is also the culmination of decades of neglect for public health resources.

Those who question the need for national healthcare are hopefully undergoing a rapid transformation in thinking right now as they see the impossibility of our bits and pieces approach to government healthcare. Just about anyone who works for a living hates the idea that non-working people could be out there getting free shit, and I understand that frustration. Government healthcare just sounds like one more thing to *pay for* on behalf of someone else. The reality is that healthcare is not always about you, but you do always reap the benefits of it. You are not paying for their benefit, you're paying for yours.

Sick people cost money. Sick people get other people sick. Sick people struggle to maintain a job. Sick people reduce productivity. Even if you're not the one using it, you're still getting a great and necessary benefit out of healthcare. If you were to go line by line through government budgets, you'll see how incredibly valuable preventative medicine is at saving public and private dollars. We should have more of it with better delivery.

Now imagine for a moment that you work in a factory and that factory has twenty human resources departments, each one doing a slightly different but overlapping thing. Not people, but rather entire departments of people.

You have noticed that your human resources budget is out of control and that it's a completely dysfunctional system. This would never have happened in the first place because it would be incredibly stupid and wasteful as a business decision. If it did happen what would be the obvious solution to fixing it? You would consolidate all of the departments into one reasonably sized department that covered all of those job tasks fully. It would be streamlined and you would cut a tremendous amount of administrative waste and staff.

As ridiculous as that scenario is, that is exactly what we have done to our national healthcare plan. Not that you should put all your eggs in one basket, but maybe if you have a few hundred baskets you could group some eggs together to get rid of a few of those. There is a fine line between diversification and redundancy. There is no reason to have so many healthcare plans for all of these different groups of people.

If Democrats really wanted to actualize healthcare reform, they would pass a bill that eliminated all of the other healthcare programs. Every single one of them, including and especially the gold-plated congressional one. Then they would simultaneously replace it with one streamlined single-payer system that covers all Americans.

This has come up before. It's not new. There was a great discussion about this in the recent debates regarding various forms of Medicare-for-all. The problem with these is that none of them swept in the other extraneous platforms. If you want to please voters and persuade Republican Senators to vote for something, offer to eliminate a few hundred thousand regulations and tackle the inflated bureaucracy simultaneously. Medicare for everyone would be great, but not if they were also still paying for Medicaid, CHIP, and every other healthcare platform under the sun. Just have one plan that covers all.

There are some major oppositional hurdles to get over to pass a bill like this. The first is a misunderstanding of what a single-payer system is.

Americans are terrified of a Soviet Union-style healthcare system where all the doctors are also government employees. Help people understand that doctors and other healthcare staff would still be privatized, they would just be compensated by the government for services they provide on the government plan. They would still retain the freedom to perform services outside of the plan.

The second opposition tends to stem from the quality of care. There is an idea that if everyone had coverage that the hospitals would be overrun and wait times would be out of control. I would like to just point out that we already have a shortage of healthcare professionals and our services are already overrun, and the wait times are already just as bad as anywhere else in the world. It's also a pretty lame excuse. If our capacity doesn't meet demand, rather than letting people just die for being poor, we could implement targeted programs that seek to improve capacity. Like education for example.

The third and most complicated opposition is that of healthcare rationing. We can probably all agree that there are many procedures that are outrageously expensive and resource-intensive. We pursue them in the private sector, but we would not in the public sphere. In a public system, the government would have to determine what is covered and how to best utilize the public's money to maximize national health. This would likely be decided by expert panels in coordination with governmental committees, kindly dubbed "death panels" in the debates over this policy because a financial line would have to be drawn somewhere on the public dime, and someone's life could hang in the balance. I would like to point out that this already happens anyway.

If it costs $100,000 for a kidney transplant, but I can prevent 100,000 people from getting Polio by vaccinating them for the same price, it stands to reason that the government would support the latter. The kidney patient stays on dialysis or possibly dies, but we prevented 100,000 other near-fatal illnesses. Americans have a huge problem with the ethics of this decision-making process. Our emphasis on individual liberty makes this a tough sell. My response to this is to consider the alternatives.

If we have a government healthcare plan but don't have a decision-making process for resource management, we could easily bankrupt the nation. Our current system of not having adequate public healthcare is killing more people than healthcare rationing would if we did have a great public health system. The existence of a governmental healthcare plan also does not prevent individuals or businesses from offering and purchasing private plans that do cover those things. All it does is sets a minimum bar for healthcare and society covers it for everyone.

It might actually cause your private health insurance costs to go down. You're already paying for Medicare, Medicaid, and all the other federal programs out of your check. This amount would likely be the same, just rolled into one agency. The difference is that you could actually access the benefits of it, instead of having to meet one of the limited criteria for use. The things that the basic federal healthcare plan covers would not be billed to your private insurer because everyone would have it. Therefore, your private insurer would only be paying for those extra things the government can't justify paying for, but that you want. That would bring down costs significantly over current expenditures because the private insurer wouldn't also be shelling out compensation for basic health services. That's the advantage of a Medicare for everyone type plan.

If everyone is paying into the government system, basic healthcare costs would go down because they could be regulated and consistently priced. The price of care need not be a fixed number. It could come in the form of block grants based on population size. It could be set to a rate that adjusts for cost of living or other metrics. There are many ways to structure this to avoid the pitfalls of a price floor-ceiling model.

Many Americans point to abuses of the current system, saying that the prices are inflated because the government is paying for healthcare. This is a valid criticism, but also showcases the need for reform. While we actually do have stringent regulations and penalties designed to prevent defrauding the system, we have very little oversight of price gouging from the pharmaceutical corporations. There has been a recent push to address this issue, but it has largely fallen flat.

When you start to compare our system to countries that have had socialized medicine for decades and analyze their prices for comparable pharmaceuticals and procedures, you find that they pay much less than we do. The counterpoint to this argument is that the quality is somehow diminished or that it makes the business unprofitable. All you have to do is cross the border into Canada to determine that is simply not true.

Canadian pharmaceutical companies are thriving. Their doctors, nurses, and hospital staff are still well compensated. If the measurement of profitable is putting a 200% markup on life-sustaining insulin so your CEO can buy a rare Wu-Tang Clan album at auction, then the Canadians are not doing well, but if you're a normal human being who goes to work every day for a living, you recognize that the boardwalk on a river of gold is paved with blood. Price controls for the beneficence of essential public health is not going to hurt anyone's real bottom line. They just might have to buy 6 luxury yachts instead of 7.

With costs under control, let us return to the issue of rationing determinations. This is the part that generates the most controversy. Not everything will be covered as we discussed, but I hope that rational people will realize that not everything needs to be. Determinations can be made as to what constitutes basic and essential healthcare covered under the government and anything else above that can be covered by private insurance.

It doesn't need to be that complicated. We spend a tremendous amount of time and controversy embroiled in arguments over things like age stipulations, abortion funding, and transgender reassignment surgery. If something raises controversy of that magnitude it's easy to just leave it out. No age restrictions, all Americans can access it, conversation done. The Hyde Amendment already prohibits federal abortion funding. If the majority of Americans don't want to pay for someone's gender reassignment surgery on the public dime, the decision should be easily made. There's no need to rope those hot topics into the public sphere and demand they be paid for by the masses.

Even if you are of the opinion that these are essential healthcare procedures, the measurement for government coverage need not be one of necessity. The vast majority of Americans can agree on coverage for things like vaccinations, prescription medications, and routine surgeries. Let that be the basis for the plan. If there are more complex services that the public at large widely agrees should be covered with minimal controversy, let's include those. Individual states can then add anything they want for citizens of their states on their state dollars.

The federal plan does not have to be the comprehensive end-all-be-all of healthcare. It just covers the essentials to keep costs low and ensure the overall public wellbeing is maintained. Individual states can develop their own rider policies for coverage of controversy paid for by their own tax base. If the majority of citizens in Oregon want to use their tax dollars towards that coverage of abortions, euthanasia, and gender reassignment surgery, they can pass bills of funding towards that end. If the state of Mississippi doesn't want to pay for those things, they don't have to. Oregon and Mississippi could probably both agree to share the burden of cost for vaccinating against hepatitis or surgeries for appendicitis. These places of mutual concordance are areas where federal healthcare makes sense. Not everything has to be federal, but some matters should be.

The opposing argument is that this creates a system that is inherently discriminatory towards certain demographics, but it should be noted that our current system already does this to an even greater degree. There is a disparity between states' ability to afford coverage. There is a disparity in different age groups' ability to access care. There is a disparity between the rich and the poor. There is a disparity in healthcare costs. A single-payer system would be the greatest step towards reducing these disparities. Democrats need to be realistic about what they can get out of this deal. Let's set aside the things that we know are going to be deal-breakers and focus on what we can actually obtain.

Research Funding

Our nation is particularly skilled when it comes to developing weapons of war. Military superiority certainly gives us an upper hand in diplomatic negotiations and gives us a greater sense of security in a dangerous world.

We spend an estimated 15% of our federal budget on military spending, but less than 1% on science. If this is a showcase of our national priorities, the ability to destroy our enemies takes precedence over our ability to create a society worth defending. That's a harsh assessment, but it's one that has become extremely obvious during the recent COVID-19 pandemic.

The number of missiles and bombs that we build which go unused is quite staggering. The argument is that we build so many of them to deter the need to use them. Maybe that works when the opposing threat is the missiles and bombs of our enemies, but much like the Trojan Horse, you can build a wall to repel an invasion, but you open the door to new problems. Problems like a national pandemic for example.

Our national healthcare infrastructure is clearly not on par with the rest of the developed world. We have the highest infection rate in the world in part because of distrust in our health and political systems, and in part, because we do not set aside enough planning and capacity to weather a crisis. A viral outbreak can completely destabilize our economy, and it's not even an intentional one. If this was a test of our national defenses, we were very unsuccessful. In the event of a real biological weapons attack, we're clearly fucked.

It has not been all doom and gloom though. When the world put itself to the test of developing a vaccine and pulled its resources together, it was able to create one. Imagine that decades of scientists have been trying to develop vaccinations for viruses of this class-type, but were not able to accomplish what was made possible in just a single year of coordinated investment. This begs the question, what if we continued this level of support and funding for the scientific research community? What else could they achieve?

We can have an arsenal of warheads, but if everyone is sick from a virus they do us little use. We should be funding healthcare and other scientific research just as much as we spend on other defense projects because they are also a necessary part of our national security framework.

Treating public health as a natural security threat would not even require additional bureaucracy. It already exists in the form of the CDC. If it is not already abundantly clear, the role of the CDC cannot be understated. Their funding is well justified and desperately needed. We should be expanding its capacity to better manage these crises.

More steps should be taken to ensure the independence of the CDC from the political fray. The CDC needs to be allowed to express its unbiased fact-based opinion on matters without contradiction from the executive branch. This is difficult to achieve, but it would be highly beneficial to structure more continuous funding for the CDC and pair it with joint private enterprises to give it a certain degree of independent revenue streams. That way the CDC can continue to operate and function as needed while protecting its objectivity. Otherwise, we risk dire consequences that result from ignorant government shutdowns and politicians who bury their heads in the sand during a crisis.

The reasoning behind federal expenditures on scientific research is multiplicitous. Healthcare projects that can yield incredible results are often large multi-state enterprises engaged in broad based testing that could not otherwise be funded or coordinated without federal support. Funding in the private sector is not always available where commercial viability is not expected. Finding the cure for a rare disease is unlikely to make you a great deal of money on the market. The federal government is able to alleviate this burden by making this research profitable to companies that pursue it. This has an overall benefit to society and advances our humanity in a way that the traditional market cannot.

Thorium - Green Energy Glows Greener

- Pass the Thorium Energy Act of 2015 or something similar.

The Democratic party has long proclaimed itself to be the party of environmental concerns. It has had long-standing goals to develop clean renewable energy sources. This is an admirable goal as our energy needs are ever-increasing, and our dependence on fossil fuels has proven to be an economic and national security risk.

The boom and bust cycles are particularly harmful to oil communities. Recall that I used to own an oilfield trucking company. We carried water to be used in the hydraulic fracturing process. Anyone who has worked in an oil boomtown knows the drill. Workers arrive for the promise of long hours and great pay, only to find themselves spending a fortune on marginal communal housing. Those who are prepared for the scams and know of the boom-bust nature of the job will ration and save their money. They come in, they make their money, and then they go home back to their real jobs, usually one step closer to paying off something.

The trouble is that the duration of the bust cycle can be severe. Those who took risks often end up going under. Companies that invested in that extra truck today, might go broke tomorrow. While hundreds of thousands of dollars flow in and out of your company accounts when the oil is flowing, a downturn can send you into bankruptcy if you're not careful. The last downturn was so bad, that the banks were saddled with collateral reclamations. Thousands of pieces of trucks and equipment sit rusting in their parking lots. In the next upturn, they became unwilling to offer capital for oil ventures because they were still saddled with the failure of their last investment. This has made it more difficult and more expensive to upstart an independent or small scale operation, a group that large and mid-size oil companies frequently rely on to fill coverage gaps in their contracts.

Meanwhile, out in the community the services and retail shops that were surging during the upcycle, find themselves without customers in the downturn. The entire economy of the area dries out, leaving its residents destitute. Eventually, the oil dries up and the trucks move out to the next location. The promise of fast money allures the residents of the next town to build upon worker housing and hotels. If you're from a boomtown, you know what happens. West Texas, Eastern New Mexico, North Dakota. They all know that you have two options. You either move up and out, or you get stuck holding the bag.

Now I was fortunate to somehow make it out alive in a state of in-between, but the recovery was challenging. I had to work very hard to overcome the loss and to this day I still retain a few company assets that just won't sell. I gradually drop my prices in the hopes of just getting it off the lot. Many others are not so lucky. I've seen folks sleeping on the couch of a one-bedroom shack just to keep a roof over their head. I've seen whole families put out on the street. Strained relationships. Suicides. You name it. I vowed to never again get my hands dirty on Texas tea. It's marked money. Business at the end of a barrel. It generates ugliness and causes pain. As a nation, we are far better off without depending on it, and we need a sensible stable transition plan for oil workers and communities who get displaced during downturns.

Oil doesn't just cause us to lose our local sense of morality. It also causes us to have some very unsavory international trading partners. We shake hands with some pretty shady characters and turn a blind eye to their flagrant human rights abuses. They have oil, they have money, therefore they make for good trading partners in the eyes of politicians. Nevermind the public stonings and lashings. Nevermind the monarchical tyranny or theocratic dictatorships. It is no wonder that the United States has lost its luster with the world on its message of freedom and democracy. Our trade policy is sweating like a whore in church. It's time that we take our reliance on foreign oil to the confession booth and take responsibility for our own energy independence.

The Obama administration focused heavily on the development of wind and solar technology. That's all well and good. Certainly domestic and renewable. Theoretically cleaner in use, perhaps not in manufacturing. The trouble is that the energy outputs are just not on par with the levels our current and future society is demanding.

The Trump administration did an optimistic 180 with the passage of the Nuclear Energy Innovation Capabilities Act of 2017. While it sounds good in theory, when you read between the lines it has little to do with the generation of energy, and a whole lot to do with updating our nuclear arsenal. No shame in that. After all, it is very important that we be able to annihilate the entire planet better than the Russians. I digress, but the bill was all uranium and no spark.

If you go back to the historical development of nuclear power technology, you'll notice that we actually had several promising routes to go down. Only one of those routes produced weapons-grade plutonium. That's the path we went down. In the 1970s we had an opportunity to expand upon it and go the other direction. With Richard Nixon in the Whitehouse, the decision to keep digging uranium was an easy one. Uranium is mined in southern California. He wasn't about to give up the green gold of his home state. He needed the state for reelection purposes after all.

As time went by and a few near world-ending calamities occurred with one still ongoing nuclear meltdown in the Ukraine, many U.S. citizens came to fear and despise nuclear power. Even the storage of decayed uranium fuel rods takes tens of thousands of years to dissipate, an environmentalist nightmare. Americans or rather the octopus overlords who rise from the remnants of the sea will stumble upon our nuclear trash even in the year 26020. It's no wonder that the Democratic Party would take a relatively hostile stance towards nuclear power. It is certainly a valuable constituent block.

The strange thing is that we know there are other ways to build a reactor. Reactors that don't result in easily weaponizable materials. Reactors that produce a tremendous amount of power in a way that does not risk a catastrophic meltdown. Reactors that don't take up as much space. Reactors that use a relatively common mining byproduct as fuel. Reactors whose byproducts decay at a significantly faster rate. I'm talking about Thorium molten salt reactors. When you start to look at this almost century-old technological innovation it leaves you with a sense of bewilderment. Perhaps if we had focused on developing instruments of energy instead of instruments of destruction our society would be in a very different place by now.

The trouble is that nuclear technology on a commercial scale is rightfully extremely regulated and highly conservative. Only the most modest and time tested improvements are made. New projects are rarely invested in and slow to take off. Probably a good thing given the incredible dangers of using uranium reactors. The Atomic Energy Act has been downright hostile to the exploration and federal funding of any nuclear project outside the narrow realm.

Efforts to amend this problem began around 2008. The Thorium Energy Security Act of 2010. The Thorium Energy Act of 2015. Both died in committee if not just read to an empty room which fell on deaf ears. There's speculation that the companies who hold stockpiles of this material derailed their own bill with competing lobbyist interests. In any event, the situation hasn't changed much, but it did receive an honorable mention from Andrew Yang, bless his infinite wisdom, during his failed presidential campaign.

There is a real opportunity here to make dramatic improvements to our national energy infrastructure in a way that is far less environmentally hazardous than any other current system being employed. Democrats have a real opportunity to do something about it, but they're going to have to be prepared to lose a few followers along the way. I will argue to the core that what you will lose in anti-nuclear hippies, you will more than make up for citizens pleased with the outcomes.

Fortunately, we don't have to guess where this stuff can be found. The U.S. Geological Survey put out a wonderful comprehensive report on known thorium veins. Among the largest of these deposits are located in Idaho, North Carolina, South Carolina, and Georgia. Three out of four of those states have seen recent Democrat inroads with candidates proving their viability. Thorium is a goldmine of opportunity for job creation in rural Appalachia. These are voters that presently have a great deal of animosity towards Democratic politicians. Making gains here could easily improve the likelihood of electoral and senate gains across the Atlantic south.

Indeed if you look at the survey map it's almost a county by county scatter plot of rosy red dots, just waiting for a Democratic President to come in and bring those good-paying energy jobs. Just plant one of those molten salt reactors out in eastern Ohio or Pennsylvania coal country with thorium rolling in from Wausau, Wisconsin, and imagine the economic and political gains to be realized.

Sure it's not entirely renewable, but it does generate high volumes of energy and it's a hell of a lot cleaner than coal, gas, or uranium. It's a victory for both business and the environment. Now granted we are still a longshot away from commercial viability, but the research and the models are incredibly promising. It's worth investigating and investing in. A powerful opportunity awaits the Democrat courageous enough to stand for a safer, cleaner nuclear. Let's get this out of committee and onto the debate floor.

Idle Cash is the Devil's Workshop: Privatize Social Security

- Privatize social security.
- Eliminate WEP

Social Security was a great idea in its time. The objective behind it was to prevent much of the suffering incurred by the Great Depression. Workers set aside a portion of their paycheck into a government account which pays them back in annuities in their old age. Workers could then retire in their senior years and have something to fall back on in the event their savings and investments had otherwise failed them. Current workers would replenish the system so that they could enjoy the benefits later while supporting those who came before them today.

One of the worst presumptions about Social Security is that the population would continue to increase at a steady rate. It never anticipated times when the participation in the workforce would be repeatedly decimated and with it the steady stream of contributions into the system. It never anticipated that people would wait longer to have children or stop having them altogether. It also underestimated how many more people would be living longer, and also how many people would rely on it as their exclusive source of retirement income. These problems have led to a deficit in replenishment for the system, resulting in less availability for future generations. At this point, most Millennials have accepted the idea that they will never be reimbursed for their Social Security contributions, and that retirement is in and of itself going to be out of reach. Hence their desire to live in the moment, enjoy life as often as they can and take on jobs that are less physically demanding.

There is a common misconception that the gap in Social Security comes from Congress siphoning funds off of the Social Security Trust Fund. This is a myth, but it's sad that it's a believable one. The funding structure has remained consistent, even as accounting has changed. There are other myths about *illegal* immigrants draining the Social Security system which is also completely unfounded. The gap is simply a matter of obligatory payments exceeding incoming replenishment. It could be repaired in two ways. Either by reducing the outgoing money, or increasing the incoming money, but both are unpopular. Both will one day be necessary and that date is projected to be within the next 20 years.

Making any changes at all to Social Security is a risky political proposition and with good reason considering how many Americans rely on it. There is also a substantial fear of loss after the 2008 recession wiped out decades of retirement savings. It is understandable why people would support the status quo. They need it to survive and others will need it in the future.

At this point, we are approaching a damned if we do, damned if we don't point. We can keep passing the buck for generations, but ultimately it's going to become an untenable system as our birth rates decline. The biggest problem with Social Security is that the money sitting in the trust is being taken out of the economy, and it just sits there. The distribution payments go back out into the economy, but Congress has even found a way to skim some tax dollars off of distributions. That doesn't change the fact that about 3 trillion dollars are being parked outside of the economy in the trust.

There were many policy decisions made by the George W. Bush adminis-tration that I strongly opposed, most of them related to the sheer volume of deficit spending. There is however a unique proposition that he made towards the end of his term about the idea of privatizing Social Security. This came to an abrupt end when the housing bubble burst and the stock market came crashing down in 2008 on his way out the door. As much vitriol as this policy stirred up with Democrats, it deserves additional consideration.

I think about many of the senior citizens in my life. They worked their whole lives, they retired. Their pensions were eliminated. Their stocks crashed. All they have is Social Security. Most of their Social Security is consumed by out of control rent prices. They made all the right choices. They were handed an amazing deck of cards, only to later find out that the cards were a magic trick and they ended up with nothing. This is the story of so many Americans and it is easy to see why the promise to "Make America Great Again" resonated with these folks.

The outcome could have been different. The age of retirement almost meets or exceeds the median threshold of life expectancy. That means almost half or more Americans die before ever getting to use those funds. These benefits are then conferred to some degree on children or spouses, but the entire game is dependent on the majority of the amount paid into the trust never being used.

I imagine what I would be able to live for today if I wasn't paying into Social Security every check, knowing that I will statistically never be able to use it. People work their whole lives to retire only to die before they get there, or be too sick to enjoy it. They could have used that same amount of money to pay bills and be less stressed out all their lives. They could have taken more vacations. They could have invested more in their assets, like making home repairs. They could have had a shorter term on their mortgage. They could have invested in businesses. They could have enjoyed more consumer goods. Instead, they are stuck making a mandatory investment that they have no options for. What exactly is Social security Securing? Given the choice of enjoying life while young and being destitute as an old man, most people would prefer the latter. It is better to live without regrets, then to live without risk.

Privatizing Social Security is a happy medium between the current system and having none at all. When you go to receive advice from a financial planner about starting up a 401K or mutual fund, you're presented with a range of products. Each has a varying degree of risk and set of targeted investments. There are high-risk funds for those who have more time to play the game and there are guaranteed funds for those who want to play it safe. In either event, their money is going towards something in the economy. That money is exchanging hands somewhere and driving the economy forward. Social Security has no such options, but there is no reason why it couldn't.

If we really look at it, the point of Social Security is to inoculate civic services from being overrun by a crisis of bankrupt seniors, and it achieves this by forcing them to set aside their money for a rainy day during their youth. Another way of looking at it is that the policy infers that the majority of Americans are not responsible enough to make their own investment decisions, so the government does it for them like the parent makes that their teenager put a portion of their check into a savings account that they control.

What I would like to see with Social Security is a range of plan options that allow for actual engagement in the economy. Even amidst multiple crises and numerous total market crashes, my 403B has seen consistent net gains over time. Imagine how much better I would be doing if all of the money I was spending on Social Security was going into that account instead. Just imagine my net worth if my Social Security contributions of ten years ago had gone into Bitcoin. If our grandparents had started investing in mutual funds with the same amount of money, they might have all retired as millionaires. Instead, their funds sat dormant in the public trust, and now they can barely afford rent.

Personally, I would opt for a high-risk plan. I still feel young enough to gamble some with my investments. My wife on the other hand is much more conservative with her spending, she would likely opt for a low-risk plan with more guarantees. The ability to make such choices should rest in the hands of the individual. If you're going to force them to set aside money, they should at least be able to set it aside wisely. If every working American is tied into the market, they have a vested interest in seeing to its success. I imagine we would see much greater accountability in business if the entire society had a stake in its outcome and direction.

I am all for programs that help people and serve the greater good, but they have to be sensible. The design of our Social Security model is not as great as it has been hyped up to be. We can and we should do better. Some degree of privatization would go a long way.

Windfall Elimination Provision

Not everyone pays into Social Security. There are state-level pensions that are used as an alternative and that same amount is distributed into those funds where the money can be invested and saved differently. Many situations arise where a worker has qualified for both; vestment in their pension benefits but also accumulated enough points to withdraw Social Security.

The "Windfall Elimination Provision" offsets the amount in Social Security benefits for people who draw a pension. The name suggests that it would somehow be unfair if you were to receive the full value of both and that it would result in a waterfall of public cash flowing into your account. Now forgive me if I'm wrong, but most of the people I know getting their Social Security benefits or their pension, are still struggling to get by. They're not rolling in money as the provision would suggest. It is one of the most ignorant propositions in all of government to suggest that because you were sensible in working multiple jobs and qualifying for multiple entitlement contributions that you should somehow only receive part of that benefit.

Full disclosure. This provision will ultimately hit me in the gut when I retire if nothing changes. I stand to lose something close to a 40% reduction in my Social Security benefits if I also draw my Teacher Retirement System pension. I paid into both systems. I deserve to be compensated by both at the rate that I put in.

Repealing the Windfall Elimination Provision has become somewhat of a campaign issue this year with President-elect Joe Biden and Senator Elizabeth Warren supporting the repeal. Hopefully, Democrats can gain the sense to make good on that promise. There are retired state and public employees all across the country in every community in America that are being hurt by this every month. If Democrats can put that 40% back in their pockets, they will be rewarded with voters.

Be All That You Can Afford: Sensible Military Funding

- Stop building frivolous surplus equipment that the branches don't need.
- Replace obsolete defense industry with scientific and technological industry.
- Limit personnel quotas based on recommendations from military leadership.
- End the practice of deporting non-citizen veterans.
- Reinstate benefits for LGBT related dishonorable discharges.
- Increase psychological care funding for veterans.
- Invest in R&D that has primary commercial applications.

Sensible Military Spending

President Eisenhower remarked in his final farewell tour that Americans should beware of the rising military-industrial complex. He argued that it would commit the United States to endless spending, escalating arms races, and nefarious influences in politics. A nation whose economy thrives off of war will inevitably find more reasons to go to war. It is hard to imagine a Republican president who was a five-star general in World War II, standing before the nation telling them to reduce national spending on mechanisms of war. Unfortunately, Eisenhower's warnings fell on deaf ears and many of his dire predictions came true.

I hear many of these sentiments echoed in military leadership today. The

Army repeatedly asks the government to stop sending them tanks that they don't use. They take up too much storage space, they cost valuable dollars and manpower to maintain, and the majority of them never see combat action. Yet they just keep building them. It is a battle the Army almost never wins. It is not that they do not have needs. There are plenty of things on the list. It's just that tanks are not one of them. However, somewhere nestled deep within a handful of influential congressional districts, there rests the infrastructure of a struggling tank factory.

It is understandable that we do not want to lose our capacity to build them and that we want to keep those great manufacturing jobs going right here in the United States. However, there becomes a point of harmful absurdity. We could look at this factory and ask ourselves how we could improve it and diversify it to meet real consumer needs. Instead, the solution is almost always to keep things just as they are. The tank company is not becoming more viable by staying in one place and the Army isn't getting stronger over it. We're just spending money and wasting raw materials to satisfy ego.

I pick on tanks because I worked at Caterpillar, the company that practically invented them, or at least the tank treads. Caterpillar did not become a Fortune 100 company by resting on its military contract laurels. It diversified into new products and new markets. When the government isn't buying tank engines, they build construction equipment. They build cruise ship generators. They build mining equipment. They build truck engines. They build tractors. They're able to do this on the same lines in the same factories because they adopted strong research-based manufacturing processes.

Over-reliance on government money can unfortunately lead companies to become less innovative. Those who are particularly skilled at producing what the military wants can often back themselves into an inescapable market niche. When the funding dries up or the engagements of war change, their business has nowhere to go. For communities that rely on these plants for their economic sustenance, their representatives become powerful advocates for the military-industrial complex. The plant becomes so integral to the community's economic success that its representatives will do anything the company wants to keep it happy.

What I wish the people in these communities would see is that they are preyed upon by these companies in many cases intentionally. These large scale manufacturers set up shop in places where they can squeeze the tax benefits out of the local populace. It creates an enormous unpayable debt in infrastructural maintenance costs for the local municipal government, but they gleefully go along with it for the opportunity to bring in a whole lot of jobs all at once. They always think that what they lose on the deal, they can make up for with the increase in the local tax base. They are almost always wrong.

The volume of new jobs created causes an unnatural growth in the town. The prices of land go up. The prices of commercial property go up. Residential property values and taxes go up. Another set of terrible decisions is made for expedient development to capacitate all of this new growth. It looks great in the beginning. A few decades later the town starts to run out of money. They can't afford the maintenance upkeep and replacement costs. Realizing they've been conned, they start to pass ordinances to recover their losses from the company. The company needed all these things to move there and it didn't deliver economically to pay for them.

The town goes to the company to collect what is owed. The company doing what every good con man does escapes from town. They leave behind a giant crumbling useless building, and the entire town falls into ruin from the job loss. The company sets up in a new town unscathed, claiming the factory was just "outdated" and "the business climate was hostile."

It's amazing how a small town can be doing great or getting along just fine before the factory but suddenly finds itself in a total state of closure and insolvency a few decades later when the factory leaves town. The conditions that were there before still exist, and they could exist again, but the community is now plagued with debt that it cannot repay, and in a total state of shock from the volume of job-loss. That's why whenever your local tank company says jump, you ask "how high?". The company only needs to say they would go under if it wasn't for the tank contracts, and *presto* the representative of the community slides it into a defense spending bill as a requirement for their vote.

What is needed is a transition plan for companies that produce dated and obsolete military equipment. Innovation would have been ideal, but it's not always possible. When it reaches the end of its term with no renewal in sight, the company needs to be phased out and transformed into something else. The alternative is doing nothing and collapsing the local economy. When an addict goes to rehab they're often given transition drugs that help reduce the shock on the body and to curb the addictive cravings in a way that causes less harm than quitting cold-turkey. We need transition businesses to exit the factory from the small town gradually. This is where an investment in science and technology comes into play.

Instead of building unwanted equipment for the military, we should invest in research and development for products that are actually in demand. I've seen numerous successful transition businesses that include things like turning an old factory into a server farm or turning the former mall into a distribution warehouse or medical park. It's not going to save every job, but it will save quite a few, and it will replace the existing infrastructure with something more functional. It just needs to be enough to reduce the shock.

However it is structured, the ultimate goal should be to break up the big box factory into smaller units. It is better to have a multitude of smaller businesses, that way if one of them goes under it doesn't destroy the town with it. The worst thing a town can do is try the same thing twice in a row. Replacing the failed factory with yet another company of the same size will delay the inevitable, but the cycle will repeat, and the community will be right back where they started. That is because communities build their economy from the ground up. The economic activity in the small town or region does not justify the factory's presence. The company's participation in the global economy does not change that.

You diversify your stock profile to mitigate risk and maximize gains, why would you put all of your investment into one company and hope that your town grows into it? This is no different than the empty pre-planned cities of the Chinese interior. It seems no matter how big it is, or how grand you build it, you can't get people and economic activity to show up just because the infrastructure is there. That is not how communities work.

In a similar vein, you cannot just hire people continuously where people are not what is needed. There is a tendency among lawmakers to try to fix economic shortcomings by creating jobs. It makes sense in theory. We hire a bunch of people to do things, we find the cash for it in an easily passable defense budget. They get paid, they pay taxes, and they spend money in the economy. They equate it to a classic FDR style work program, but it's easily distinguishable. Those work programs were performing essential services to the domestic economy that were either in actual demand in the community or added value to the community. More bodies building more bombs does not necessarily achieve that.

This is a frequent problem in the Air Force. In times of modern drone warfare, it is not about the quantity of people you have enlisted, but rather the quality and skills of the people enlisted. They frequently find themselves with a wasteful excess of staff in certain areas while having critical shortages in other areas. Congress hinders their ability to function cohesively by putting too much intervention into personnel management.

Envision this scenario. Congressman Bob says the Air Force must hire 10 people to fill the Major's coffee because that's what people in his district know how to do and his cousin Bill needs a job. The Air Force in turn goes to Congress and says they don't need any of those people, but they desperately need a robotics programming specialist and there's no money for it in the budget. Congressman Sally is upset because her district is already shelling out the big bucks for Bob's coffee fillers. She brokers a deal and gets personnel shifted around to allow for the new specialist position, but it comes with the stipulation that it has to come from one of Bob's coffee fillers.

Bob is a nepotistic sack of shit, and Sally is a dumbass because you can't just turn a coffee filler into a robotics programming specialist overnight, but nonetheless, we're stuck with them because they keep getting reelected somehow. The next time Bob and Sally go to write a bill, they should probably talk to the Major first. He can fill his own coffee, but he sure could use that specialist. Instead of telling him what the military needs, they should listen to what leadership within the military says it needs. Maybe the next time he needs to fill a specialist position, he shouldn't have to go to Congress to get it done. This is an extreme simplification of matters, but if you break down what actually happens, that's a pretty fair representation.

That is the main point behind all of this. We have experts with lifelong careers in the military. They know what we have. They know what our enemies have. They know what we need to stay on top. There needs to be a partnership of trust and understanding between them and the people writing laws for them. Cut the pork fat and spend money where it's actually needed. We'll get Bob's cousin a useful job that's actually in demand and supported by his local economy, and we'll rescue the smalltown from it's tank factory conundrum, but we're not going to use the military-industrial complex as means to an unnecessary end.

Democrats can be anti-war, pro-military, and fiscally responsible at the same time. It just takes a great deal of listening and understanding. Companies that are successfully producing the modern equipment our military needs should continue to get contracts. Companies that have fallen into obsolescence need a transition plan. The military knows who they are. The congressmen in these districts know who they are. Understand the motivations and fix the underlying problems. Most decisions have multiple right answers. The decision to not build tanks because they don't need them is an easy one. Deciding how to best support the people who were making them, is complicated but it's not impossible. Leadership is finding a way forward.

Taking Care of our Veterans

I came to be good friends with one of my dad's girlfriends. She was a Republican from California who had run a diverse gamut of careers from agriculture to aviation. We often had cordial discussions about matters of politics and law. She introduced me to a group in Tijuana whose sole purpose was to support deported U.S. veterans.

The very idea that someone who had served our country and volunteered their life for our flag could even be deported is astonishing, but it is sur-prisingly more common than you would like to believe. It often stems from drug use charges, which is even more unfortunate because their use typically stems from untreated PTSD incurred because of events in the military. Not only did they serve, but they also experienced something awful and instead of giving them our help, we threw them out.

This should not be a partisan issue and it should be immediately rectified. The mechanisms of causation for the deportation of veterans needs to be carefully reexamined. This power should be reserved exclusively for those who commit foreign espionage and saboteurs, not a minor drug conviction. Military service has long been a proud traditional means of obtaining U.S. citizenship and that pathway must continue unencumbered.

Deported veterans are not alone in their struggle to access services and benefits to which they are entitled. In 2016 I was working on my master's degree at Texas State. My professor was pretty incredible and she often coached others in the community on writing books. She brought in a guest lecturer one day to tell her story and it was incredibly impactful to me. Her name was Alice Hoffman and she had just written a book about her life and was promoting a cause near and dear to her, the plight of LGBT veterans during and prior to the "Don't Ask Don't Tell" era.

She went around the nation collecting the stories of LGBT veterans who were dishonorably discharged on the basis of their sexuality, and their families. This discrimination had long-lasting repercussions. It hurt their future employment prospects. It restricted their access to benefits of all kinds. Their partners were likewise barred from access. They volunteered their lives to the defense of their country only to have their country shit all over them. Many of them were dishonorably discharged under other charges that they were not guilty of because in the eyes of their superiors it was less detrimental to them. This has only made it more difficult for them to challenge these assertions in the future. Alice talks about her experiences of having to hide and mask her identity for such an extensive part of her life as a career servicewoman.

A few months later, I saw her again at a local bar. She was raising funds for her cause, so I made a donation to the jar and we had a chat. She organized a public awareness campaign whereby she was going to bike all the way from Los Angeles to Washington D.C. from sea to shining sea, stopping along the way to tell the story of LGBT veterans. She actually did it, having several people join her along parts of the route. Upon reaching D.C. most members of Congress could not be bothered to meet with her. There was one who was willing to listen, Senator Bernie Sanders. He listened to her stories and offered his support for restoring the rights of LGBT veterans who had been discharged. From there, I've heard nothing additional about the movement, but I suspect Alice is still fighting an uphill battle to capture the public's attention.

Democrats take the LGBT community for granted. They get a ton of support and money from them, even when the politicians deliver very little for them in return. It's obvious where Republicans stand on LGBT issues and that leaves them with little alternative but to vote Democratic. This won't last forever though. Democrats have been lucky because LGBT Americans still hate Ronald Reagan for his handling (or rather lack thereof) of the AIDS crisis. Eventually, this will be forgotten and so will Republican opposition to marriage rights. They'll forget. The young will probably know nothing about it. If Democrats do not stay active in doing *for* the LGBT community, they will find themselves losing a critical voting block.

The next time Alice goes to D.C., I hope that more Democrats will listen to her cause, and seek a practical remedy for the past harm done and prevent this from happening again in the future. America's military should be as diverse as our nation and we need to do more to defend them as they have defended us.

While we are on the topic of doing more for our veterans, it is imperative that we discuss the ongoing mental health crisis and the incredible lack of resources devoted to this problem. We put our soldiers through a very intensive training process. We give them highly demanding jobs, and there are times when they experience the unimaginable horrors of war.

There has been a resurgence in interest in psychological care for veterans, and I hope this enthusiasm is sustained. Research continues to make breakthroughs in our understanding of PTSD, our ability to produce prosthetics, and our ability to heal wounds of both body and mind. Unfortunately, many veterans are still unable to get the care that they need in a timely manner.

There have been many newsworthy situations that have occurred when a soldier's mental health burdens become too great and they snap, often harming themselves or others in a dramatic fashion. I would much rather tell the stories of those whom I know because it is far more prevalent than the isolated incidents that end up on television.

One of my friends enlisted in the Army shortly after we graduated from high school. It wasn't that he was all that service-oriented or even patriotic. It just seemed like a smart career move. College wasn't working out for him and the economy was heading off a cliff and into the Great Recession. The Army was shelling out fairly large signing bonuses at the time. It was a great option. I think that he hoped that the military would bring some sense of purpose and community to his life.

Lots of people enlist because they were promised a military that would straighten them out. It was going to fix your life, give you discipline, cure your mental health problems, and make you a better person. You could reach your highest potential. Most officers would likely say the same thing because they were probably more well-adjusted than they thought they were going in. Maybe it does work for some, but for others, it only compounds their problems. Recruiters are getting wiser about this, but during times when recruitment becomes challenging, they tend to bring on some people they really shouldn't.

After basic training, my friend came out on the other side looking great. He was enthusiastic. Ready to take on the world. He was promptly shipped overseas to support the war effort in Afghanistan. It's difficult to imagine that twenty years later we would still be over there fighting the same war, to the extent that most Americans no longer know if or when it ended.

He returned from his tour of duty relatively unscathed. He was quite satisfied with his choice and had even discussed the possibility of reenlisting. It seemed that all he had been told was true. Unfortunately, he had picked up quite a serious alcohol habit and was already a heavy smoker, but that is a relatively common affair for young people in general.

Just as things were looking up, a horrible series of events unfolded. He ended up falling in love with a fellow soldier. Workplace relationships are always frowned upon, but especially in the military. It's actually quite common and it makes sense, these are the people you are always surrounded by.

There is a great deal of stress that comes from such a relationship. They kept their silence about it and concealed it as best they could. For all the regulations and cautionary tales, I think every soldier has at some point known or at least had some inclination of romantic relationships in the military. Sometimes between officers and their subordinates. If asked about it they would tow the company line and say regulations prevent it, but in reality most of the time they stay silent and let it be their business. They don't want the drama or the controversy and there is a deep sense of duty to those in your tribe. They keep it like a family secret.

One day my friend was off-base having some drinks with a few friends. As they were crossing the street, a drunk driver collided with his partner. He died in his arms. Imagine that you have survived all the horrors of war only to be killed on the streets of your own country. It was quite a traumatic experience, made even worse by having to keep his silence even at the funeral. He fell into a deep depression and began abusing drugs. As it was not a war-related injury and didn't happen on base, there was not much thought given to his wellbeing. Not that he could really talk about it, the matter had to be kept secret.

It was during this time that he was sexually assaulted by another service member, making matters much worse. He reported the incident to his superior, but he was shamed and ridiculed for coming forward. This is also unfortunately not an uncommon occurrence. Progress has been made on this front over the past decade or two, but the military still remains a fairly hostile work environment for many people, particularly women and LGBT servicemembers. Some branches and bases more than others.

As I said, relationships are forbidden, but not uncommon. Most cadets are teenagers when they enlist. While their peers are exploring their sexuality in college or in the workforce, the cadet is constrained by circumstance. Rigorous training and shore leave have little impact on biology. When you combine this with the isolation of war, pre-existing mental health conditions, and a culture of aggression, it becomes a recipe for some pretty complex problems where people engage in behaviors they might otherwise restrain themselves from whether it be romantically or non-consensual. A similar phenomenon is observed in prisons. Something to consider...

After undergoing an evaluation my friend was promptly diagnosed with a generic mental health condition and honorably discharged. The solution to the problem was to just make him go away as quickly as possible. Out of sight out of mind? The love of his life was gone. The job he loved was gone. All that was left were the problems and the suffering. I might have been the only person to truly know him and it took him an entire bottle of whiskey for him to get through the story enough to tell me about it.

My friend ended up living in a rundown part of the city, sharing an apartment with several other drug users. He tried several times to get help from the V.A. hospital, but care was infrequent, insufficient, and slow. The Obama administration really made a concerted effort to try and fix these problems, but it just did not materialize fast enough to help my friend. He eventually lost his battle with heroin and passed away.

The last time I saw him I just happened to run into him on the city streets. I waved to him and asked him how he was doing. He was quite emaciated. It was like only his body remained, but his soul had departed. He just stared at me as he passed by never really acknowledging that I was there. It was like he was not really there at all, just a dead man walking.

Those who defend our country deserve better. It is not just those who see combat who experience trauma in the service. It is not just those who take a bullet who are injured in the line of duty. I hear similar stories all the time from people of all branches and walks of life.

Congress ought to be forced to use the same healthcare system as veterans. Imagine how different it might be down at the V.A. hospital. This should be an issue easily agreed upon by Democrats and Republicans alike. Physical wounds may heal and you might never know they are there, but emotional pain remains. Our veterans need more long-term mental health solutions. This includes expedient access to care and a lifetime insurance benefit to pay for it. Whether they were ever deployed or not.

Tough on Rights: Criminal Justice Reform

- Eliminate voter restrictions on the incarcerated.
- Eliminate or reduce reliance upon parole systems.
- Take steps to reduce hiring restrictions based on criminal records.
- Equal funding for prosecution and public defense teams.
- Implement restorative justice programs.
- Ban solitary confinement.
- Eliminate the death penalty.
- Ban private prisons.
- End the appointment of justices.
- End the practice of lifetime appointments of justices.
- End foreign trade with countries that commit human rights abuses.

We have one of the highest incarceration rates in the world. An outside observer might think that we either lived in a crime forsaken hellhole or a paradise where all the criminals had already been arrested. The reality is that our justice system is fundamentally flawed and desperately in need of substantial reform. When your justice system becomes the injustice itself you have lost the ability to proclaim that you live in a civil society of law and order.

I went to law school believing as most people do that I was going to help people. I thought I could be a champion for social justice and that the problem was that we just needed more lawyers who cared. Three years later by the time I graduated my taste for law had soured. I couldn't bring myself to be a part of a system that I so fervently disagreed with.

There was a time where I got into juvenile justice after meeting a highly dedicated and charismatic public defender. I sat in on a few trials and volunteered to do some legal research on behalf of Judge Jean Boyd. It was pretty gut-wrenching to see wave after wave of young teens, almost always teens of color being sentenced over what used to be considered trivial offenses. Smoking dope behind the gym used to earn you a trip to the principal's office for a stern lecture. Now it's a felony that they send kids to prison for. That wasn't always the outcome, but that never should have been an option in the first place.

Then something remarkably appalling happened. A childhood friend of mine was on her way home from a catering event. She was probably in her early twenties and she had just opened a successful catering business. It was her dream and she was living in it. Her car broke down on the side of a country road not far from her home. A bystander had come to her aid along with some friends of the family. As they attempted to get the car going again, 16-year-old Ethan Couch was driving drunk, three times over the legal limit. He killed four people including my friend and injured nine others.

The case ended up in none other than Jean Boyd's courtroom. Given the conflict of interest, I quit volunteering there and stayed out of it expecting justice to be rendered. This would become the infamous "affluenza" case. Couch came from a rich family that bought him a strong legal defense team. He basically got off with a slap on the wrist because the judge was persuaded by the argument that he was somehow mentally incapacitated by his wealth. The family lifestyle of consumerism had somehow made him crave more and more riches to the point that it drove him to a state of high anxiety that led to his drunken manslaughter spree. Basically, it was complete bullshit that has no clinical or even logical basis.

The public was understandably outraged. Boyd responded to critics by saying the public didn't have all the facts. Had she been more attuned to the community she might have known that everyone knew the facts. While brown kids in Tarrant county were getting tossed in jail for petty theft, Ethan was going to end up at a country club psychiatric facility for spoiled brats.

No justice for the victims and it sent a terrible message that you could buy your way out of jail even if you killed somebody. Needless to say, she wasn't a judge much longer.

Couch of course violated the conditions of his parole by of all things drinking alcohol at a party. I'm not sure what is worse, continuing to drink after your drunk driving murdered someone, or having friends that will still party with you after you do. He and his mother disappeared into Mexico fashioning almost comical disguises. They were apprehended and returned. Couch was sentenced to a whole two-year sentence. Two years after his release he violated his parole again by failing a drug test.

That is only one of the millions of examples where money and race influenced the judicial process to grant favorable treatment. We've seen it all the time. Rich criminals building their own private prison wing to stay in, complete with tennis courts. Meanwhile, the majority of the accused who cannot afford an attorney spend an average of five minutes with their public defender before trial. Imagine making decisions that impact the rest of your life in five minutes.

Equity for the Public Defender

If you hang out around criminal courts long enough, you realize that there is a massive disparity in the time and resource availability of the appointed defense attorney and that of the prosecutor. Public defenders tend to be fewer in number and almost always get paid less than the prosecution team. The argument is that the prosecution needs the additional resources because they have a higher burden of proof. The reality is that only about 3% of cases ever make it to trial. Most of them strike a plea bargain.

There is nothing inherently wrong with a plea deal. It saves judicial time and resources. It's expedient. The accused admits their guilt or accepts the penalty anyway and negotiates a sentence. The judge typically rubber stamps it, and there's no need for drawn-out expensive trials. In many cases, the evidence is clear and definitive and often the defendant knows they have nothing to gain by contesting it at trial.

In reality, this can have devastating consequences. Defendants who accept plea bargains are often not properly counseled on their rights or the extended consequences of their admission. There are even times where the judge throws out the plea and issues a harsher sentence than what was agreed to. Other times people admit to crimes they did not commit, just for the convenience of getting it over with.

With my disgust for law at its height, I decided to become a teacher. If I couldn't help kids once they were in the system, I could at least try to keep them out of it in the first place. I called it "practicing preventative law". It's the short polite answer to the question of why I became a teacher, because describing everything that is horribly wrong with the justice system doesn't make for good teacher's lounge coffee talk.

We were taking an exam one day and I noticed that one of my A+ students was just going to blow the whole thing off. He had no motivation to even start it. I pulled him aside after class to talk about it. He told me that he probably wouldn't be there much longer. I asked him what he meant by that. He told me that he would likely be in juvenile detention for a few years.

He had been arrested over the weekend and accused of stealing lottery tickets and cigarettes from a convenience store. He told me that he had been nearby the area when it happened and was just walking home. I asked him about his trial and what he planned to do.

His appointed attorney met with him after his arrest and in just a handful of minutes had advised him to accept a plea deal when he returned for his trial date. The kid didn't even have a suit. He told me he had just planned to go in and plead guilty. I asked him why he would want to do that. I'll never forget what he said next. "I'll probably just end up in there anyway. People who look like me always go to jail". His confidence in the justice system was so low that he presumed that he was going to be incarcerated no matter what the truth was. At 14 years old he already had this somber awareness.

We stopped by the campus social worker and got the kid a suit for court. I gave him a five-minute crash course in court decorum and told him to ask the prosecutor to present him with the evidence before he signed the deal. Something any defense attorney, court clerk, or paralegal could have done. It's not even a matter of law that he needed to be advised on, he just needed someone to tell him to stand up for his own rights and how to act right in a courtroom. His attorney was in such a rush, he just assumed someone else would advise the kid on what he needed to do. No one ever did.

He goes in to meet with the prosecutor and asks for the security tape from the convenience store. Almost every store in America has one. The prosecutor had to recess to conjure up the tape by calling up the store owner. They had never even reviewed the tape. When they finally played it back for him, the thief clearly passed by the height bars on the door, placed there precisely for the purposes of helping identify criminals who steal. The thief was a full two feet taller than the kid standing before them.

Needless to say, the case was dropped right away. This kid was about to sign his life away. He was about to go to jail for a crime he didn't commit, on the advice of an overwhelmed, overworked, underpaid public defender who had not even bothered to look at the evidence. It was an absolute injustice of the highest degree. The police made no effort to investigate. The prosecutor just presumed the police had given them the evidence they needed to make the conviction. They drafted up the standard brown-kid-goes-to-jail-agreement, and they shipped him over to the public defender to rubber-stamp it.

It is hard for me to fault the public defender here. His caseload was in the thousands. Imagine being tasked with keeping track of so many cases you don't even remember the name of your client because you're reading it off their case file on the day of trial for the first time. People sign terrible pleas all the time because they don't get the attention and explanations they need. There are so many secondary penalties. You might think you're doing good pleading guilty to a certain offense if you can avoid jail time until you realize that once you do, your criminal record haunts you the rest of your life. Depending on the state any number of consequences could be incurred. Can't get a job. Can't get a professional license. Can't live in certain places. Can't get government benefits. Can't get financial aid for school. Can't vote. Can't adopt. All because you smoked a joint at the park once? It has to end. We need to restore value and respect to the public defender's office with equitable resource access.

If we have so many cases that we cannot provide effective public defense counsel, then we have too many crimes. Justice is not void of economics. I would rather that we dropped a number of crimes from our books than to side-step the Constitutional rights to counsel.

Secondary Consequences

The purpose of incarceration in the United States is primarily punitive. While it would be ideal to have a more restorative incarceration system, we have yet to really pursue that with any serious integrity. Under this model, your time in jail is time served. It's the price for the crime committed. Our Constitution is designed to prevent the notions of double jeopardy and the application of cruel and unusual punishment. Among the interpretations of meaning assigned to this is the notion that the punishment must be fit to the nature of the crime.

At the inception of our government, these rights did not apply to slaves. When slavery was ended, the emergence of Jim Crow laws sought to transform the justice system into a second institution of slavery. You could no longer restrict the rights of a Black man on that basis alone, but if you accused him of a crime, his rights were easily revoked in prison. As a result, a number of secondary consequences emerged around the incarceration system. A prison term had to fit the crime, but sentences could be extended under the guise of a parole system. It could be extended for behavior during time served. It could be extended in the form of unpaid fines. Through a variety of mechanisms, the deprivation of Black rights could be extended.

When these systems are exposed for what they are, they have evolved to further mask their overt racial injustice. The inception of the War on Drugs was one such example. The entire "tough on crime" movement is just another excuse to deny people their rights in perpetuity. Our justice system today is largely complacent with these secondary consequences. Propaganda has very successfully indoctrinated the public to the idea of "once a criminal, always a criminal". This is counter to the entire stance on jail as effective compensation for time-served. They presume the criminal will re-offend, and they design a system that all but ensures that they will.

One of the most egregious violations of liberty is that incarcerated individuals lose their right to vote, sometimes even after their release. The justifications sound compelling enough. If we allow criminals in jail to vote, they could elect someone from within the jail who will release them all. Governors and Presidents could exchange pardons for votes. They might overwhelm the town and elect leaders who would repeal the statutes under which they were convicted.

Before you allow yourself to agree with that notion, ask yourself this question. Why are there so many people incarcerated within your jurisdiction that they make up a sizable and decisive voting block? If you have that many prisoners are they really criminals, or is the law unjust? I'm inclined to say it is primarily the latter.

A counterpoint to this argument is that prisoners are concentrated where the prisons are located, so they would make up a majority in those districts. This could easily be solved by continuing to allow the prisoner to vote in the jurisdiction of their last known address. Then if you still have that problem, you know the law is what is wrong and needs to change.

Here is how these voting restrictions came to continue. You cannot Constitutionally stop a Black man from voting. You can, however, stop a felon from voting. All they had to do was design a series of felonies that they knew would target Black men, and then tailor a system of policing to enforce it. Despite a few decades of conscious social awareness about this phenomenon, little has been done to change anything. Hence why we are seeing so many examples of blatant police brutality, murder, and subsequent protest movements.

At this point in 2020 incarceration for what I call petty felonies, such as marijuana possession, are not only violations of racial justice, they also amount to forms of political imprisonment as well. In recent decades Black voters have overwhelmingly voted Democratic in numbers as high as 93%. Hispanics likewise have been voting in numbers as high as 70% for Democrats. While Black Americans make up only about 13% of the U.S. total population, they account for almost 40% of those incarcerated. Hispanics to a lesser degree make up 16% of the population but still account for 19% of its prison population.

This is an issue that Democrats need to take more seriously. Whether intentional or not, incarceration is disproportionately happening to Democratic voters at the hands of Republican lawmakers. A racial disparity of that magnitude does not occur by accident. Republicans continue to stand in opposition to the restoration of felony voter rights because they are well aware that the people they have incarcerated are primarily Democrats.

It was amazing how quickly the public accepted the recent narrative of riots. We have seen incredulous abuse of power against Americans exercising their First Amendment rights to peaceably assemble in protest. Tying all protests to a handful of riots has given police virtually unrestricted discretion to engage in warlike actions against U.S. citizens in their own country and has led to thousands of unjustified arrests. The majority of those arrested have been Democrats and leftist organizers engaged in lawful peaceful protest. It is political suppression in plain sight.

We have even seen the latest Republican administration invent a fictitious leftist enemy of the state labeled as "Antifa." They have used this premise to harass, detain, and imprison their political opponents including numerous Democratic grassroots organizers. This is not a deception of the media, I have seen with my own eyes the arrest of prominent local civil rights attorneys on the Margaret Hunt Hill Bridge as they participated in legitimate, legal, and peaceful protests. It is happening everywhere.

These are the kinds of things the United States would impose sanctions on another country for doing. Democrats absolutely must take aggressive action towards eliminating felony restrictions on voting rights

Interestingly enough, this is something Democratic mayors actually have the most control over. There must be a coordinated effort among mayors to withdraw their police forces from engaging in these nefarious arrests. This goes far beyond diversity training programs. Substantial reform is needed, particularly in how resources are allowed to be distributed, and what actions the police force is allowed to pursue. Mayors have a surprising amount of leverage over such matters and Democrats have almost unilateral mayoral control over the nation's population centers. You can "back the blue" by making it a better institution. Continuing to look the other way while these injustices continue is only going to make matters worse for both citizens and the police force.

On that note, kitsch slogans like "defund the police" may be empowering to the user, but most voters find them to be a turnoff. The average voter responds best to Democrats when they are direct and they say exactly what they mean. Instead of repeating a mantra, tell the people what it is that you as a candidate intend to do and frame it in a way that demonstrates a partnership in improving police and citizen relations.

You are reallocating funds towards more social programs to reduce the likelihood of criminal activity occurring in the first place and to foster better relationships between the citizens and their police force in order to build mutual trust and understanding. It's safer for officers and better for the people. If you scream "defund the police," whether or not you actually believe that or not, a sizable group of must-win Democratic moderates hears "kill good-paying jobs." You cannot expect to run on a kill the jobs platform in blue-collar America and expect to win.

The next problem in the chain of secondary consequences is hiring restrictions imposed on former inmates. Again if we truly believe that punitive justice works then there should be no reason to continue punishing inmates once their sentence has ended. If prison worked, they must be cured of their criminal ways right? The second a criminal record shows up on your background check it becomes infinitely more difficult to get a job, and certainly not one of merit.

Inmates are often released with no plan and no resources. If they have no friends or relatives to take them in where do they go? No bank will lend you a mortgage. The majority of apartment complexes won't sign a lease with you. Shelters won't take you in. You don't usually have transportation. Then it is practically illegal to be homeless in most places. Your only hope is finding a halfway house with some availability, or by some miracle, you were part of a work-release program and have enough funds to get on your feet.

Most places require that you have a physical address to be employed there. This is not necessarily the fault of the employer. If you've ever had employees from different states you know what a pain in the ass it is when you go to file your payroll taxes. Many employers won't take the risk of an improper tax filing, so they won't hire you without an address.

There are special tax incentives in some places for hiring former convicts. If you are fortunate enough to land one of those jobs they usually pay rock bottom wages. Most often it is through other convicts that they are able to find work, which places the newly released convict in situations that potentially violate their parole or puts them in the path of their former negative influences. Then once they do finally obtain a job it becomes almost impossible to get a promotion, irrespective of the quality of their work ethic or skills.

Entire classes of jobs also become off the table. Obtaining a state career license is virtually impossible, even if the nature of the job has nothing to do with the crime committed. I understand that if you wrote a hot check that you might not be the best candidate for a financial advisor license, but that shouldn't necessarily be a disqualifier from getting a cosmetology license.

As a result of these problems, former inmates tend to end up living in the same communities. They usually end up impoverished. They have few opportunities for upward mobility. They cannot get government services. They cannot get assistance to reeducate themselves for new career fields. This in turn harms their families as well. Their best option under the circumstances is to re-offend. We have practically designed a system that encourages it because there are few options outside of drug dealing, prostitution, and theft. Almost half of all former inmates end up back in jail within a year, not because they wanted to keep being criminals, but rather because it was the only option they had left.

There are some truly heinous crimes out there. People are understandably distrustful of criminals and want to be cautious in hiring them. However, there are also plenty of people who went to jail for just a handful of months for a petty crime and in many states, they are treated the same as murderers who just got off of thirty years. Reasonable states have crafted legislation that exempts certain crimes from being evaluated on background checks. More states need to do this, but it becomes exceedingly difficult in the toxic

"Tough On Crime" Era.

The more secondary restrictions we impose, the less likely an offender will be able to reintegrate into society, therefore making almost every sentence a life sentence. This stands in opposition to the Constitutional principles that we claim to stand for. With a 44% recidivism rate, it also seems exceedingly clear that fully punitive justice accomplishes very little.

Most people do not wake up one day and decide to become a criminal. There are of course some deeply disturbed people and those with compulsions, but the average criminal is just an ordinary person who was dealt a bad hand in life. The primary causes of crime include; anti-social values or personality, negative peer influences, a dysfunctional family life, substance abuse, and challenges with self-control. Any educator of merit can tell you that these problems are almost always correctable if the right person intervenes at the right time. This is as true for kids in school as it is for adults. Sometimes people need help and have no one to turn to. While we're getting justice for victims, we need to also be taking steps towards reducing the likelihood they will offend again, but we also need to take steps to prevent the formation of criminals in the first place by expanding our social services.

Restorative justice can be highly effective for both criminals and victims. Research studies have shown that it can reduce recidivism rates by almost half. If we truly want to reduce crime, why do we continue to ignore these statistics? Look at the countries that have adopted restorative justice programs. They all have demonstrated reductions in crime.

One of the most egregious crimes to happen in Norway in recent memory was that of right-wing terrorist Anders Breivik who killed 77 people. In the United States, this would unfortunately probably be a one-day news story that lasted until the next mass shooting death. In the case of Norway, he single-handedly raised their annual murder rate. They practically had to build a new prison just to house him. His lifestyle in prison is in many ways better than most people living in the United States today. Maybe we don't want to go that far, but we should be asking ourselves why the Norwegians have one of the lowest incarceration rates in the world.

The reason they have been so successful is because they treat their criminals similar to the way a doctor treats their patients. They analyze the symptoms of the crime and they seek to prescribe a remedy. Throwing someone in jail as mere punishment accomplishes nothing on its own other than removing them from the population and making the victims feel restored. Sometimes that is what is needed and serves a just purpose. For most petty crimes it just makes things worse. Prison typically only exacerbates the underlying conditions that led to their crime. They will be out within a few months, and they will just be worse off than before if nothing is done to help them become something else. You must address the underlying causes of the crime to make the crime go away. While we have prisoners isolated from society and under supervision, we should be making more productive use of that time.

There are numerous restorative justice programs out there that have proven to be effective. Democrats need to educate themselves on programs that work and secure funding towards implementing those. I know a lot of Republican lawyers and I can assure you that there is very little interest in getting this done across the aisle. While they're screaming "lock'em up!" just keep pushing the success rates and express your goal to do things that work. In order to sell it to the public, frame it economically. Incarceration costs money. Recidivism costs even more. Nothing backs Republicans into a corner like promoting a policy that saves the public money.

Cruel and Unusual Punishment

A civilized society does not need to impose the fear of torture and death to deter and control crime in its population. Our Founding Fathers were keenly aware of this and were sensible enough to write it into our Constitution. Fortunately, they even failed to define it with any detail so that it could be changed in response to future societal tastes.

It is time for us to make an updated revision on how we treat prisoners in our custody, based on what experts in psychology and criminology have recommended. Solitary confinement comes in many colors and I will use it in the context of children first. When a child has a violent fit of rage, the recommended remedy is to first remove the other children in the classroom away from the incident before addressing it further. This leaves the child in a form of solitary isolation. Another form of solitary isolation comes in the form of separating the misbehaving child from the classroom by sending them to a more controlled setting away from the other students, like the principal's office. Students that are prone to violent outbursts can also go to designated locations to self-isolate and cool off momentarily. These are all temporary measures of isolation. Now imagine the controversy if you were to lock a child alone in a closet and leave them there for days, weeks, months on end, sliding food under the door periodically. Most people recognize that as a severe form of abuse. Why is it acceptable to do that to adults in prison as a form of keeping order?

Solitary confinement is a form of torture. Humans are social creatures. Without some form of meaningful human interaction, we become mentally unstable. Many people in prison are already mentally unstable and solitary only makes matters worse. As a temporary measure to separate an inmate from an altercation that might be an acceptable use, but continuous indefinite isolation is not necessary to maintain order.

Based on the nature of their crimes and the suffering of their victims many Americans turn a blind eye to this. They might say that this is what they deserved, or that it is not far enough. If you've ever met a group of protesters outside of a criminal proceeding you hear all sorts of cruel forms of torture that they would bestow upon the criminal. It is a natural inclination of the public to be angry when something unthinkable has happened.

This disorderly mob rule of order is precisely what a statutory justice system is designed to prevent. Solitary confinement is a stray torch and pitchfork. Government imposed torture, no matter how well deserved it may be, can only lead to an unsavory abuse of power. Democrats should seek to reduce the time allotted for solitary confinement or discontinue its use altogether. It is not the most popular policy change, but it is necessary for the preservation of liberty. There is no reason to go that far though, you can just say we're going to do it because that's what experts in this field are recommending and we value expert opinions.

That brings us to the next torture of consideration. The death penalty serves a dual purpose. The first is to stem the tide of mob rule. The second is to rid society of particularly vile offenders and attempt to deter future people from doing the same. Clearly, it has not been that effective as mass murder and crime continues unabated.

It is estimated that somewhere around 5% of inmates in the United States were wrongfully convicted and are actually serving time for a crime they did not commit. Given our extraordinary rate of incarceration, this amounts to somewhere between 100,000 and 150,000 inmates sitting in jail while they are actually innocent. After working with the Innocence Project in law school, I am convinced that the number is likely even higher than what is estimated.

I remember serving on a particular committee that prescreened letters to determine whether the facts presented merited a reexamination of their case before presenting it to an attorney. It's a great way to spend a Thursday afternoon, and I think every law student should try it if even for only a few sessions. I was truly astonished by what my peers were willing to turn away on the basis of feeling or intuition. Our goal was to impartially evaluate the merits of the facts as they were presented, not to determine whether they were true. I cannot tell you how many rejected applications keep me awake at night. I can think of nothing worse than being convicted of a crime you did not commit. It destroys every aspect of your life. Your family, your friends, your reputation, your liberty.

At the time of this writing, there are 2,553 on death row in the United States, waiting for their turn to die. That means there is an estimated likelihood that 128 of those on death row are there for crimes they did not commit. Maybe those sound like a good margin of error to statisticians, but we're talking about state-sanctioned murder. Imagine how you would feel as they strapped you into the electric chair knowing deep down that you did not commit the crime. That is what 14-year-old George Stinney experienced on June 16th, 1944. As the United States was liberating concentration camps in Poland, they were executing Black children in South Carolina with malice and reckless disregard for morality, decency, and due process.

No system of law is going to be perfect and for that reason, the death penalty cannot be ethically imposed. The more time you spend with lawyers and judges, the more you realize just how often they get it wrong. It is not always accidental either. There have been countless examples of corrupt prosecutors planting false evidence to achieve higher conviction rates or incompetent defense attorneys who derailed their client's trial. I cannot in good faith justify the use of the death penalty when the system is so ripe with abuse.

I recall having a candid discussion with a frustrated family law attorney. In his mind, his client had completely derailed her child custody hearing based on new photographic evidence that the husband was bringing forward. She had taken boudoir photographs of herself engaged in a fairly common sexual fetish involving BDSM. Her husband had possession of the photographs, no doubt because he had probably been the one who took them for her. In any event, he was planning to present the photographs as evidence that she was a sexually depraved maniac who was going to expose the children to all matters of deviancy if left in her custody. A bold proclamation from a man who frequently beat his wife in front of his children. "Have you guys ever heard of such a thing?" the attorney asks me and the office receptionist. He was genuinely shocked by the practice and felt he should discontinue his representation with her.

The receptionist and I both look at him unphased. She pulls up a website on her phone and casually explains to him that it's actually extremely common. He brought in a licensed sex therapist as an expert witness and the pictures were excluded from the case.

That single five-minute conversation dictated the course of this woman's life and that of her children. If we had not been there to hear about it, and knowledge of the practice, she may very well have lost the case. Things are not always as they appear and there are many cultural misunderstandings that go unaddressed in law. Sometimes it is not ignorance of the law that leads to wrongful conviction, but rather an ignorance of culture and custom.

I think of it as the shadows of two people behind a sheet. To the observer on one side of the sheet, their activities might look suspect and evidentiary. On the other side of the sheet, someone has merely bent over to get a flashlight. If everyone involved in the process is only able to see the other side of the sheet, they're going to get the wrong conviction and no one would even know.

Discovering applicable law is easy. Presenting facts in their best and truest light is an art form. Jurists are not so much selected as they are farmed. In order to win your case, you lead the juror out into the pasture and show them the field, so that they don't see the slaughterhouse in the barn. It is not always clear what is really happening when the facts are framed.

We like to think that we have heightened scrutiny for death penalty cases, and surely they would be reserved for only the most egregious criminals. Reality says otherwise. It may not be as overt as George Stinney's one-day racist murder trial, but we're still getting wrong. Likely to the tune of 128 people per year. Even if the slaughterhouse in the barn is an illusion, it only takes one juror to think they saw it to convince the others that it's there. If your buddy Earl saw a ghost once, well it's highly likely that you did too. Not only that but yours was bigger. A jury of your peers is often no better than a single judge. Flocks will ultimately follow shepherds. That doesn't make them just.

Democrats should seek a nationwide ban on the death penalty and run a state by state campaign to ban it in state criminal courts as well. Politicians often skirt on this issue because they believe it will make them look weak on crime. There are numerous religious denominations that have denounced the death penalty, including Catholics who make up a considerably large voting block in most states. Forming a coalition around this issue is not as difficult as people think. Just remind them of the time the government electrocuted a 14-year-old boy to death after wrongfully convicting him because he was Black. Whatever bullshit excuse they have to endorse the death penalty after that is between them and God.

No civilized nation should allow the possibility that its government would knowingly and deliberately murder its own citizens whether they were awful criminals or not. That brings me to another consideration. There are many countries out there in the world that have no such prohibition on cruel and unusual punishment and actively commit heinous human rights abuses in broad daylight. The United States has friendly diplomatic relations with most of them and we consider them valuable trading partners. We even send them aid money from time to time.

The wealth of our trading partners should be measured in the liberty they provide their citizenry. A nation can be overflowing with riches and resources, but if it lacks basic human decency and ethics, it is a toxic barrel. There is nothing in this world that is worth trading for that would convince me it was necessary to turn a blind eye to these violent displays of public execution and beatings. Prisoners are being tied up and lashed until they bleed, pass out, or die. They bury women in the ground and throw stones at them until they die. Prisoners are being decapitated or having their limbs amputated by swords. It is not even that these people committed egregious crimes like mass murder. They did things like steal a loaf of bread. Graffiti on a subway station. Slept with someone outside of their marriage. Existed as a homosexual.

There is no consumer product on this planet worth allowing these acts to go unchecked.

Americans are currently at a heightened state of frustration over global trade on issues of fairness. They are seeking a return to a more insular economic environment predicated on localized trading and self-sustainability. Capitalize on the opportunity to make trade as moral as it is lucrative.

Blue-collar workers are incredibly suspicious of foreign trade. They feel that they are losing their livelihood to foreign workers who are paid a servant's wage to economically undercut the American workforce. The pandemic has illuminated severe restrictions in our supply chain in the midst of a crisis because we are so heavily in bed with foreign manufacturing. They want jobs and production to return to America.

It is not necessary to cut off foreign trade entirely. Globalization is a reality of our modern world. Who we choose to engage in global trade with is entirely within our control.

The United States is fond of pushing its agenda abroad. Nothing talks more than money. Democrats should pursue a trade policy of morality. Fair compensation for workers. Equitable trade balances. Only trade with nations whose laws respect human rights.

Our current trade policy reflects the cowardice of our government to say no to its own corporate executives. "They're a powerful ally in the region," they say. "We have substantial investment holdings there." I have heard countless excuses made for why we should buy oil from monarchies, and none of them are good.

This may be news to some politicians, but money doesn't vote, people do. Trust me on this that there are far more people who are not executives than those who are. I challenge a Democratic candidate to go down to Odessa-Midland and tell a group of roughnecks that you're going to cut off trade with [insert foreign nation that beats its citizens with sticks here]. They'll probably start clapping. Now deliver the bad news. Tell them that it might hurt their investment portfolios abroad and that it could cause Giant MegaCorporation to go under. Then after they're done snickering about how little fucks they give about that, tell them that we'll experience a temporary resource shortage that will require us to drill a lot more of our own oil. Move on that shale like a bitch. When you're an oil rig they let you do it. Grab'em by the refineries.

Your opponent will get a fat donation from Giant Megacorp, but you don't care because you just ushered in a blue wave in Texas. If your perceptions are only based on what those at the top of the industry say that they want, you're alienating a huge swath of voters. Never lose an opportunity to talk to workers on the shop floor. They'll tell you everything you need to know about a company.

Judicial System Reform

You can pay me to imprison people for you and I'm going to keep the difference in the profit I gain by reducing the costs. If that sounds like a fucked up proposition that's because it is. The term "private prison" should never have come into existence. There is nothing more dangerous than attaching profit signs to inmates. It astonishes me every time I think about it.

It is not a matter of if or when private prisons will corrupt the justice system, it's already happened over and over again. Judge Mark Ciavarella Jr. was a county judge in Pennsylvania. He was convicted of accepting over $1 million in bribes from a company that specialized in developing juvenile detention centers. In exchange for the bribes, he sentenced kids to those centers to boost their profits. It was fondly named the "kids-for-cash" system. This went on for a period of six years, and after it was discovered, the Pennsylvania

Supreme Court ended up vacating around 4,000 convictions and the judge was sentenced to 28 years.

Remember when I was saying the death penalty was a bad idea? A single judge wrongfully convicted 4,000 kids, threw them in jail, and ruined their lives just so he could get some extra cash that he probably didn't even need. Imagine if it was the manufacturer of lethal injection drugs bribing the judge.

If the government cannot afford to incarcerate all the people breaking the law, it should have fewer laws. If it cannot afford the maintenance of its prison facilities, it should release prisoners. Turning to private corporations sounds good in theory. It streamlines operations and incentivizes cost-saving solutions. Except, these leeches are profiting off of crime and human suffering. It's completely immoral and unethical.

Imagine a bill comes up for criminal justice reform. Your state has wisely decided to consider adopting restorative justice programs. An independent assessment of the bill estimates it will reduce incarceration rates by 30%. The private prison lobby comes for a visit, complete with its grim reaper robes and sickle to kill the bill because it would hurt their shareholders. Imagine that a corporation would lobby for more crime and more incarceration because that's how it made money. You don't have to imagine, this really happens.

Democrats should ban private prisons nationwide. Better yet we should all pass a Constitutional Amendment to make this ban permanent. Absolutely nothing good can come from them. It's the lousiest way I can think of to try and save a buck.

While we are on the subject of bribery and judicial corruption, it is worth reconsidering how our judicial system is structured. It is so commonly accepted for executives to appoint justices we don't even question whether it is a wise policy.

It is a power typically reserved for the President or the Governor. Essentially the CEO of the government gets to appoint its own board of directors. When dividing and separating powers, we repeatedly decided it was a good idea to let the potential dictator we're trying to avoid appoint their own judiciary. When FDR passed the New Deal and it wasn't sitting well with the courts, he immediately began to realize that he could just keep appointing judges until they agreed with him. The same proposition has emerged recently in response to some of the most contentious SCOTUS nominees in history. As much as we may like the New Deal or want Joe Biden to keep appointing justices until we get everything we want, that's not necessarily a positive outcome for the nation.

There was, however, one interesting concept to note about FDR's infamous court-packing plan. He was specifically targeting judges over 70. The complaints of the past are the same as they are today. There is and has always been a staggering difference between the values, needs, and opinions of the youth and those of the elderly.

In our present circumstances, necessary reform is primarily being obstructed by people in this over 70 category, and as much as I love my grandma, I'm not sure that she should be making landmark court decisions that affect the rights of someone in their 20s. It's not that I don't value her wisdom and opinions on certain matters. It's that the world is so fundamentally different in every possible way from the time period she grew up in to our present day. There is a reason why retirement was invented and it wasn't just because of infirmity. The upcoming leader of the free world is 78, he is succeeding a man who is 74, and he has to make economic policies that support a tech-based gig economy. Perhaps FDR wasn't wrong to reconsider the idea of lifetime appointments.

Justices could be elected. The purpose behind their lifetime appointment is to inoculate them from political pressures to free them up to make better impartial judicial decisions. The reality is that we have created a court without any real accountability. We have an 8 year maximum cycle time on presidential administrations. We could just as easily achieve the same goal as the original intent of the Supreme Court, but limit the terms of justices. I would suggest something like a 16-20 year term. Enough to oversee at least one more executive administration cycle, before they have to be reelected again.

The media is already quite fond of grouping the Justices into "liberal" and "conservative" categories. I can think of dozens of cases where the Justices have been in absolute discordance with these labels. In some cases it was constructive, in other cases, it was disappointing and non sequitur. Despite all of the effort to remove them from the political cycle, they become central to its dialogue anyway.

Lifetime appointments become problematic because they allow judges to supplant their own individual opinion for cases without any real checks and balances on their decision. We have been programmed to tolerate this concept of the judiciary. If the Constitution says it, then it must be a good idea. Nevermind that bit about slaves or prohibition. The Founders were visionaries, but that doesn't mean they were always right. Decades without accountability has led to some absolutely absurd judicial outcomes. It allows Justice Thomas to sit on the bench and ask no questions in oral argument for years on end. It allowed Justice Scalia to invent his own nonsensical version of judicial interpretation and now his two predecessors have adopted it as their own. The Court has even gone so far as to declare corporations people.

It is of course a necessary prerogative of the Court to render unpopular, though necessary, decisions in defense of the rights of the minority and with respect to the Constitution. We would not want a system where decisions of necessity could be overturned by a near term election of an angry mob. That being said, we also cannot sustain a nation on the opinions of the elderly alone. As beloved as they may be, can we realistically expect someone in their late 80s to be rendering decisions that impact how the nation uses computers?

The world changes fundamentally within the span of a century. We are comfortable with setting minimum age restrictions for becoming lawmakers because we recognize that age and experience have some bearing on the operations of complex systems. We also recognize that as people reach a certain age, they start to decline in health and capacity. It leads to the awkward dinner conversation about when it's time to take grandpa's keys or get rid of that revolver in grandma's purse. It is no different than our hesitation to put a 15-year-old behind the wheel of a car, yet we have no age maximums in civic offices. We absolutely should.

When the public feels a judge has reached the end of their tenure and decides that it is their time to take their keys, they presently have no recourse. All we can do is wait and watch wondering if we will ever restore sensibility to the Court within our lifetime. The present trend would suggest I certainly won't live to see it, but I would like to see future generations of Americans have the opportunity to recall a judge when it's time for them to leave.

There is a parabolic curve to judicial decisions of controversy. The decision stirs the hornet's nest and the population speaks out or acts out in anger. Then within a manner of just one or two election cycles, the decision is usually forgotten. A 16-20 year term would still allow for that cycle to continue. However, there are certain decisions that proceed in a linear or exponential fashion. The public disagreement is so powerful that it begins to consume the political system, but there is no recourse for the judges who made that decision. We all just sit there in our agitation waiting for the moment they decide to retire and hope the right person is in office to replace them.

If we want to analyze this using Justice Scalia's bullshit Originalism Doctrine, if we look at what the Founding Fathers were thinking when they chose a lifetime appointment model, the average person only lived to be about 40 years old. It is unlikely they ever envisioned a Justice lording over the bench for five decades.

Introducing even a modest form of judicial election system does not necessarily change that outcome. A popular justice could continue to serve for five decades if that is the mandate of the people. I just believe that people should have the option to choose otherwise. There are currently 13 Circuit Courts. In fairness to the divergent ideas of our populace and with respect to the protection of the minority, we could elect our Justices using the jurisdictional boundaries of those Circuit Courts. A court of 13 individuals who would better represent the totality of the body of states could surely render far more agreeable decisions than our current lot.

We could easily extend this to our 94 federal district courts, and to all of our state courts as well. In Texas, we are quite fond of electing our judges. For decades there was a longstanding unspoken rule that all judges ran as Republicans here regardless of what party they actually supported. Similarly, in the heavily Democratic districts, the judges would all run as Democrats. That is because reasonable judicial candidates decided that partisanship interfered with objectivity and was detrimental to the institution of justice. An ideology that has since been forgotten in this state for better or worse. It stands to reason that we could enact sensible legislation that eliminated party affiliations for judicial candidates. Inoculated from party politics, but still at least somewhat accountable to the public by way of elections.

Before you find staunch disagreement in what I just proposed, I want you to consider how you feel about the Affluenza judge. She was just a local judge, but imagine if she wasn't. Imagine if Ethan Couch had made his appeal all the way to the Supreme Court, and the Justices agreed with his too-rich-to-go-to-jail defense. The public would have absolutely no recourse for that decision, absent the extraordinary measure of electing a court-packing President. The Justices would continue to serve their life terms and that decision would rule over America for generations. If that sounds as awful to you as it does to me, let's do something about it.

Democrats are currently and rightfully irate about the Republican hypocrisy of obstructing the judicial nomination process whenever it suits them. It stands to reason that they are the most poised to make changes to the system. If President Obama was disallowed from nominating Merrick Garland, President Trump should have been prohibited from nominating Amy Barrett. Lawful but awful. If we elected our Justices, none of this would have ever happened. Neither of them would be on the court.

Just consider for a moment the controversy of Brett Kavanaugh's nomination. I have never seen a worse judicial nominee mired in more controversy. Given that there are thousands of well-qualified candidates, there is no reason to select candidates that huge swaths of the public outright disdain. Kavanaugh would never have made it through an election cycle in any Circuit, and we all know it. Why do we then allow such atrocious policymaking to continue unabated? It's time for systematic reform of the Court at the Constitutional level.

Purple Mountain Travesties and Fruitless Plains: Agrarian Reform

- Relax import restrictions on ruminant species.
- Fund the farmer, not the farm corporation.
- Reduce work-visa restrictions for agricultural laborers.
- Promote heirloom seeding and crop diversification.
- Subsidize the American cider industry.
- Commit more national resources to forest conservation and wildfire prevention.
- Establish a new National Park at Allegheny National Forest.

It has been a while since we heard much about agriculture in this country. We've heard discussions about whether or not to install price floors. We've heard the plight of fruit pickers and migrant workers. We heard about how Trump's trade policies were fucking over soybean farmers. Having spent a great deal of time off the beaten path, I can tell you that those things are not what you will hear most people in rural communities talking about. My goal here is to address the things that I do hear about, but I rarely hear politicians say and offer up some solutions for those problems.

Relaxing Import Restrictions on Ruminant Species

The word ruminant likely has many city people rushing for the Google search engine. Texas has long been known for its cattle industry. We love our steaks medium-rare, and many still uphold the cowboy lifestyle. Plenty of folks who just dress that way for no reason too! What you may not know is that Texas is also a huge market for the goat industry. Ruminants are a class of animals that include goats and sheep.

These animals are near and dear to me. My grandparents kept goats on their farm almost exclusively. I still have my great grandmother's famous goat brisket recipe, and I assure you there's nothing else quite like it. Not only do they make great lawn mowers, they're also delicious. Not all goats are bred to be food or lawnmowers. There are ruminants whose fur is used to make fabric, like wool or cashmere. There is all manner of goat's milk products on the market with soaps being quite popular in boutique markets.

There was a time when I pursued a dream to become a goat farmer myself. My friends used to make fun of the Meatgoat Handbook that sat on my coffee table. My students used to joke with me about what I would do if I came into a pile of money. I told them they would see me around town with an unkempt beard, wielding a shepherd's staff, dressed as Moses and tending to my flock of Boer goats. The ever-increasing cost of land was somewhat of a deterrent from ever actualizing this dream. My wife also threatened to slaughter me if I bought her a goat and then auctioned it off to be eaten. It was a well thought out compromise that if I couldn't eat my goats, that she couldn't bring a chicken into the house.

The ruminant industry has not taken off like many other agricultural commodities, despite its ancient history of being tended to by humankind. For thousands of years, humans have cultivated ruminant herds for their survival, using them for all matter of products; clothing, food, shelter, soap, bone tools, musical instruments, etc.

Today you would be hard-pressed to get the average American to try goat or mutton. Most fabrics are synthetic blends. Our building materials are more permanent now. Yet Americans will happily snag a hamburger and toss the bones to the wind. This is something we should reconsider for the sake of our economy and our environment.

Cattle farming is among the leading causes of greenhouse gas emissions in the agricultural world. They produce a tremendous amount of methane.

Cattle require higher feed yields than ruminants and they are harsher on the soil. Cows are grazing animals. Their feeding practices rip the roots from the soil, and they consume the valuable resources the soil needs to replenish that grass in the future. This means if you're not bringing in food for your cows, you're constantly having to move your cows to new lands as you reseed. Goats on the other hand are browsing animals. They consume underbrush and weeds, which actually can help improve the vitality of the soil because it removes those nutrient draining plants from the system.

A goat requires less space and I can fit far more of them per acre than cattle. They're also significantly more portable for transport. I can simultaneously transport goats with much greater ease and efficiency than cows. Any adult that can toss hay bales can likely also pick up a goat with ease, but I don't know a single person who can pick up and move an adult cow. In this era where Americans are becoming more conscious of sustainability and self-sufficiency, ruminants should be at the forefront of these discussions. I know for sure that I could not sustain a cow in my backyard, but I'm relatively certain my neighborhood could support a self-sufficient flock of ruminants. Why aren't more people talking about this?

Ruminants actually face heavy import restrictions. Considerable fear has surrounded the importation of goats and sheep due to outbreaks of a variety of diseases. Caution is certainly advisable. The quality of care has also been an issue. Ruminants are prone to numerous parasites, which has become an increasing problem for veterinarians to solve. Many would-be goat farmers quickly find themselves upside down in goats. By failing to cull their flocks, they end up with overcrowding, diseased, genetically deficient goats. The law has tried to intervene to prohibit poor farming practices to reduce the likelihood of a pandemic crisis. That is understandable. However, the law is also punishing responsible and knowledgeable owners by restricting their ability to import new stock.

The limitations on imports have actually led to the very problem that they sought to prevent. With a restricted stock of ruminants to choose from, we have seen a major decline in genetic diversity. Inbred ruminant populations tend to suffer from amplified recessive trait abnormalities. In order for the market to increase in viability, we need the ability to exchange breeding stock to prevent this problem from occurring. It is entirely possible for us to craft sensible import laws that account for herd safety but still allow for additional stock to enter the country.

Democrats want to know how they can reach rural voters. Have a serious conversation about goats. Listen to what people in the industry have to say about their needs. The greatest part about goat farming is that goat farming operations are almost always local. The giant megacorporations tend to stay away from ruminants. If you want to reach real people in real communities, who really engage in family farming activities, look no further than your local ruminant auction house.

When a presidential candidate comes to Toledo, they go to Tony Packos, they sign a hot dog bun, and they interact with locals. They do this because they know that is what is required to win there. It doesn't sound like an essential campaign stop, but everyone knows that if you don't stop there, you don't win Ohio.

When a Democratic presidential candidate comes to Texas, they miss every essential stop. They always end up at rubber chicken fundraising dinners in Austin. Austin is already voting for you, you don't need to go there. Those are not the people who need to get to know you. Those are not the people whose vote you're going to need to win. If you want to get serious about winning Texas, go down to San Angelo on a sale day. Don't go there to talk about what you want to do for them. Go there to listen. Find the places where you agree and discuss how your policies can be better aligned with their needs. Know your goats, know your grains from your oats, and you can win rural voters from coast to coast.

Fund the farmer, not the farm corporation.

Farming is certainly not what it used to be. My great grandfather could balance his coffee mug hanging out the window of his milk truck as he made his way down the winding delivery road. Small family farms used to make up the backbone of every nation on Earth. Knowledge and technological advances have transformed the way we do agriculture. Cities have ballooned as farms become larger, more consolidated, more productive, more technologically integrated, and require less labor. Inevitably this has forced many of the smaller localized farm operations to incorporate, change everything they do, or fade away.

There is somewhat of a battle that wages in the farm policy community. Who gets to call themselves a farmer? What constitutes a family farm? Has incorporation helped or hurt the farmer? When you start to talk about who is a small business it becomes a matter of perspective. To the backyard chicken farmer, a closely held 10-share farm corporation seems enormous. Those people may be looking up to the multi-state firms saying they're the big guys. You ask them and they point to the multi-national farm conglomerates and shrug. All of them are struggling to make ends meet in their own way and their problems are diverse. It's easy to look up and think you've found the source, but that's not necessarily a productive solution or a fair assessment of the issues they are facing.

Once the cat is out of the bag it is hard to put it back in. We have a very cavalier image of the farmer who lost the family land to the tendrils of the greedy banks and getting swallowed up by the giant farm corporation. It makes for a great Hollywood blockbuster. Unfortunately, we're far beyond this point now. That ship has sailed. In the span of two to three generations, the majority of Americans no longer know where their food comes from. They have no idea what the struggles of today's farmers are or what to do about it.

This has become readily apparent across all matters of industry during the last round of Coronavirus stimulus. It was almost entertaining to watch the speed at which the small business loan programs were depleted. Companies that some might consider to be huge were shamed for taking money away from what people felt were the *real* small businesses. The problem with shaming the company is not realizing that they were authorized under the conditions of the bill to do that. It was Congress who was in error. Many of them are so wealthy and so deeply entrenched in multinational corporations that they look at a restaurant chain like Chilis and think that's what a small business is. From their perspective their right. That doesn't mean they're pursuing good policy or helping the average American by doing it.

When I was just starting out my trucking company, trying to get my feet off the ground, I learned very quickly that the law is very bad at distinguishing between a megacorporation and a two-man operation. I always wanted to be in compliance and run my business ethically and to the letter of the law. Those who had been in business for a while told me I would go broke before we even got the keys in the ignition. They all said the only way to make it was to ignore the regulations and hope for the best. If you got caught the fines would probably put you under, but if you paid the licensing fees, taxes, and registrations you would also go under. It was a lose-lose situation. I cannot say that they were wrong.

There was little to no discernment in the law. A few hundred dollars here and there is fine when you have a fleet of one-hundred or one-hundred thousand trucks rolling 24/7. For the independent operators that cuts into a huge portion of the bottom line. What for them amounts to less than 1% of their expenditures, would cost me somewhere between 25-40%. Everyone has their hand in your jar, and you can't help but wonder why they're after your pennies when the guy next to you is raking a pile of cash on his front lawn.

You do not even get the illusion of a fair chance at competition. The unfortunate reality is that these types of companies do not actually compete. These two-man mom and pop shop businesses do not even register on the market share percentages held by a megacorporation. The demand is there. The need is there. We filled the contract overages. We took on the small haul jobs. We're not all billionaire venture capitalists who can ground-start a megacorporation. The law nonetheless treats both businesses the same.

This all goes back to one of the greatest problems in government. For some reason, we're very uncomfortable with legislation that acknowledges the reality of differing needs and differing means. Even when we try to do so, it tends to fail. We have a progressive income tax structure, but my grandmother on her fixed Social Security income paid more in taxes than the President of the United States did last year. What is the point of making logical distinctions in size and means only to carve out exemptions that render it pointless?

Farms are no different. Each size tier of farm has its place in the market. We cannot just throw money at it generically and expect to fix the problems. Large agricultural enterprises are more concerned with trade tariffs and restrictions. They have global logistical problems. Large domestic producers have to coordinate a multi-state distribution network. They are more concerned with biofuel regulations and genetic patents. Small farmers are more concerned with local ordinances and imposing tax and regulatory burdens that they cannot afford to meet.

The small farmer must often structure their business around specialized niche markets. Heirloom seeds, exotic breeds of livestock, fur trade, rare herbs, artisan cheese, etc. Their risk burden is much higher on an individual level. Small errors have huge consequences to their business. Nonetheless, they provide essential and desirable products that the big companies won't assume the risk for. They need different tiers of support and laws that allow for that distinction.

Given our propensity for being bad at making determinations of fairness in competition, it makes more sense to provide direct aid to the actual laborers of the farm industry rather than to the business entities themselves. No matter how large in scale the business and operations side of farming gets, it is still a land-tied enterprise. I can uproot an unprofitable factory and relocate it to a new city elsewhere. I can't do that with a cornfield. I either have to change the use of land to support a more profit sustaining enterprise, or I have to sell that land. The land itself isn't going anywhere. On the other hand, a profitable piece of land will continue to be produced upon regardless of whether a giant corporation controls it or not. When a farmer says they are struggling or they are hurting for resources, it is tied to a localized need, even if the source is a global problem. If you direct the aid to the farmer, they can spend it on what they know that they need to sustain their local operations. If you just hand it all over to the business entity and tell them to spend it wisely, you run the risk that the farmer's needs will continue to go unmet. After all, the megacorporation is already not meeting it.

If the megacorporation as an entity is such a great and profitable use of agricultural land, then its individual members can invest their aid money back into it. I doubt it would be spent that way. The corporation is just a set of ledger lines trading fake money. The real labor is happening on the farm. It is their livelihoods that are at stake if their land fails to produce a profit. That is what we are ultimately trying to protect, whether you are in a one-man band, or an orchestra. Don't protect the entity, protect the person. They are the ones who vote. Let the farmers decide which entity they want to invest it in. If they keep it all for themselves, you have your answer about the value of farm megacorporations.

Reduce work-visa restrictions for agricultural laborers.

It is no secret that the United States has a major domestic labor shortage when it comes to labor-intensive agriculture jobs. This is particularly true when it comes to fruit pickers, who work long grueling hours in the hot sun for what amounts to very low wages. The current H2-A visa program is disrespectful to the quality of labor provided and demonstrates that anti-immigration hardliners have clearly missed the boat on how jobs are created in this country.

There is nothing quite as entertaining as watching a morbidly obese Social Security recipient shouting obscenities at a news camera about the *illegals* taking their jobs. It is clear that they would be highly unqualified to fill such a job position. Americans are not willing to work a job like that for the wage it pays. They're also not willing to raise the wages to make the job more attractive to Americans because their food costs would skyrocket. Otherwise, we wouldn't be doing it. We need to stop giving the rhetoric of nonsense a platform and focus on sensible immigration policy that meets our needs as they exist in reality.

The H2-A program on its face looks good. If a farming operation cannot recruit domestic labor, it can bring in migrant workers on a temporary basis. They come in for a period of up to three years and then return to their home country. The company can file to extend the visa and bring them back again, but there is a mandatory waiting period. It's among the least restrictive means of legal entry into the United States, but it's still not quite meeting our needs.

The reality is that this becomes very expensive, particularly for certain states and crops. A substantial number of migrant workers are struggling financially both in their home country and in the United States. Imagine if you make minimum wage or less at your job, and the government requires you to take a three-month international vacation every three years. If you are coming over from Mexico to southern California, that might not be as problematic, but what about apple pickers in the state of Washington? That starts to become an expensive trip.

Think about your present employment. Imagine if your most valuable and experienced teammates were frequently gone for months at a time, and you're not sure if they're actually going to come back. It can be quite disruptive to your work environment. This is the kind of instability and uncertainty that H2-A introduces to the market.

The choices become, expensive leave of absence, overstay the visa, or the company has to shell out the money to send them home and bring them back. Cumulatively, these visa lapse periods total up to billions of dollars in lost revenue for U.S. farm operations. In order to offset these costs, the reality is that a substantial number of migrant laborers choose to overstay their visas and continue working anyway. There is also no pathway to citizenship through the program and there is certainly no pathway to citizenship for those who have overstayed their visa.

The work these migrants do is of critical importance to the U.S. food supply. They hold steady employment. They're integral to their local economies. They pay sales and property taxes. They ask for almost nothing in return, and despite how hard their job is and how little we pay them to do it, they still want to stay here for some reason. These are the kind of patriots we want joining the ranks of America. They deserve a pathway to citizenship.

There is a great opportunity for bipartisan consensus around this issue. Democrats have the opportunity to alleviate the social problems and ex-ploitations incurred by the current visa system, and Republicans have the opportunity to save American companies billions of dollars every year. Cost savings that might actually be able to create jobs that Americans want, instead of the jobs they pretend are being stolen from them. The conversation about the need for reform need not hinge upon the migrant themselves, the measure can be easily justified under a dollars and sense approach.

Promote heirloom seeding and crop diversification

Let me first clarify that I have nothing against genetically modified plants. I had the privilege of working in a genetics lab as an undergrad. I understand the technology and the processes that go into producing these plants. I am familiar with the benefits conferred by genetic modification. I do not anticipate that their use will diminish and I believe that they will continue to have a place on our societal table indefinitely.

I do not share the same fears or concerns that many do about the prospects of genetic harm done to humans through the consumption of GMO plants, though I do have some reservations about our use of pesticides. If you have been around farm people long enough, you've seen the long term damage that a variety of chemical agents can cause to the human body. That is more of a recent phenomenon. Human manipulation in plant genetics goes back thousands of years; terraced rice fields, the existence of maize, Gregor Mendel and his pea plants. Rather than adapting to the environment around them, modern humans have taken an innovative approach to adapt the environment to suit their own needs. Making plants healthier and more resilient so that they provide bigger harvests is a part of the human experience.

I am advocating for heirloom seeding for a very different reason. In any science experiment, there exists a controlled variable. While I am manipulating the other variables, something must remain the same as a basis for comparison. There is a reason why your word processor has an undo button. Sometimes you screw up so badly, that you need to go back to the original template and start over again. Heirloom seeds are our failsafe mechanism. We keep them in a natural state with minimal intervention. This allows the plants to retain their original genetic diversity and also allows them to continue their natural evolutionary trajectory.

We frequently discuss genetic diversity in the context of endangered predators. The homogeneity of the cheetah puts it at risk of extinction due to its inability to adapt. If your species becomes too well adapted to its environment, it can actually backfire, causing you to become less adaptive if something changes. We need to be thinking about agricultural crops in the same way. As certain seed strains become oversaturated in the market, they become vulnerable. All that effort that went into producing homogenous yellow corn, could be decimated by crows and locusts adapting in response to our modifications and pesticides. The threats to our crops are also in the evolutionary battle of their lives. When we push too hard on the genetic modifications, we also create a forced rapid adaptation of the other inhabitants of this Earth who feed upon them. Heirloom seeds give us an undo button. They give us a range of genetic diversity to return back to in order to start over or add new modifications.

We are also seeing a secondary problem with our man-made crops and livestock. In our effort to make 300lb chickens with 8 legs, we have also accidentally made chickens with tough tendons and fat deposits that make their meat less desirable. If you've eaten an orange in the past couple of years, you can taste how much the flavor has diminished over the years. A bacterial greening disease nearly wiped out the commercial viability of oranges, which has had scientists rushing back to the lab. This could be avoided if we had more diversity in seed lines.

American consumer habits need to change when it comes to produce selection. The homogeneity of the produce department is void of taste and has the potential for disastrous consequences if seed lines become too narrow as a result of it. I advise investment in public advertising toward accepting fruits and vegetables of different shapes and sizes. If you approach this from a financial and food security perspective, you will get greater buy-in than if you endorse the talking points of anti-genetics conspiracists. Have an honest conversation about the science, about the risks, and the points of mutual beneficence.

The Norwegians have made incredible strides towards the preservation of global genetics with the establishment of the Svalbard Global Seed Vault, built in 2008. They currently have around one-million samples. The work that they do is truly incredible and cannot be understated. Hopefully, more nations decide to adopt some of these ideas to ensure a higher likelihood of preservation. Our future civilizations may very well depend on these seeds and the genes stored therein.

In the United States, heirloom seeding has taken on a more local character. These are typically grown by smaller independent farms and gardeners. It would be beneficial to expand this practice and offer some form of monetary incentive for providing this essential service.

In addition to genetic diversification, the United States should reconsider its bread-basket model of agriculture. We have learned a great deal about crop rotation and soil maintenance since the time of the Dust Bowl Era, but when you look at the distribution patterns of crops today, you see the vulnerability in it. Massive corporate farms growing field after field of the same thing presents a strategic problem that we've known about for almost a century now.

Soil conditions and climate create natural geographic restrictions for crops, so we can expect to find large accumulations of certain types where the soil and weather are suitable. These pockets have become more concentrated as corporatized farming in the global market has become more specialized. While it's great to have Idaho potatoes traveling all across the nation, filling up your gas tank with Iowa corn, and baking bread from Kansas wheat, what happens to your state if its staple crop fails? We spend a great deal of time preparing for logistics in the food supply chain with respect to a major environmental or national security event, but what are we doing to preserve the crop itself? You cannot deliver the produce if there is no harvest. In this age of global warming related climate changes and threats of nuclear war, we should reconsider how we plan to sustain crop diversification in the future. A state by state model is problematic.

We have become so reliant on this that there are few if any self-sustaining cities in the United States. We rely exclusively on a global supply chain. One that can be easily disrupted in the event of catastrophe or war. Even with the best planning for delivery, how might we account for something like a pandemic, a trade embargo, a nuclear strike, or an electromagnetic surge? Sorry, but the world's supply of bananas no longer exists? Is that the world we want?

It does not have to be a matter of logistics if the food source is at or adjacent to the market locations they serve. We need more local agriculture distribution, and that is going to mean greater crop diversification and more coordination between local farmers on production. It will also take some innovation in building design.

Living in San Antonio, you might notice that access to green leafy lettuce is a rare commodity. We could say that the consumer habits just prefer iceberg or cabbages, but the reality is that even in great refrigerator trucks and rapid delivery, the lettuce just doesn't stay fresh in the heat once it's been picked. I cannot begin to tell you how many bags of salad I've had to toss because they're wilted and browned before I even got it home from the store. It would seem ignorant to try to grow shade plants in San Antonio. An outdoor plot of winter vegetables would certainly fail. However, on a smaller scale in hydroponics warehousing or greenhouses, it becomes possible. These are not giant operations by any means, but they can help supplement local market demand in the event of disaster. While there is little market incentive to do this, there is a security and risk management interest in doing this.

In the event of a crisis having local suppliers can be extremely beneficial for the continuity of economic activity. Imagine if we converted all those abandoned shopping malls into crop diversification centers that grew off-season plants and exotics. No need to send refrigerator trucks all across the country, you just ship it from the warehouse to your local grocer. That way when a pandemic bacterial disease wipes out all the orange trees in Florida, we've still got orange trees in greenhouses all across the nation still producing. If a meteor strikes in Yuma, we can continue to put salads on the table.

Botanical gardens across America have really been leading on this issue by showcasing edible plants as ornamental gardens. I'm personally very fond of the idea. I tore out the dying non-native bushes planted by my friendly neighborhood developer thirty years ago. I replaced them with local desert plants. I conserve a ton of water that way. My plants have medicinal properties and service the natural pollinators in my community. No maintenance whatsoever. They look better than the parched dying old bushes.

It was a huge win. I transformed the useless flower beds of my backyard into a massive herb garden. Indeed I have often dubbed myself as the Johnny Appleseed of the mint plant. I spent years cultivating my own hybrid blend that thrives as a delicious ground cover that repels insects, smells nice, and makes for a great tea.

If everyone in the suburbs tore out their useless grass from the lawns that they don't use and started growing heirloom plants of productive, edible, or medicinal use we would have much greater national security. Notice I keep coming back to that. When you frame it as a national security issue it brings a level of interest to addressing it that otherwise wouldn't be there.

It also gives you greater Constitutional leverage for dealing with it at the federal level. Local grass ordinances are dangerous to our national security. Our front lawns are making us vulnerable to crisis when we could be allocating those water and fertilizer resources to more productive uses.

Climate change is too politically polarizing to use as the crisis culprit, but you can use a series of fringe fears among suburban voters to push for change. Communists, terrorists, nuclear bombs, zombie outbreaks, etc. People are actually much more likely to respond to a non-existent threat then they are a real one because it's psychologically easier to handle.

In summation to this point, we need genetically diverse crops. We need old seeds as a failsafe. We need a better geographic distribution of crop diversity. We need to change public opinion about their selection of produce and about how they utilize their suburban lawns.

Subsidize the American cider industry

While we are on the subject of crop diversity, it is essential that we talk about how Prohibition destroyed a major agricultural industry. It only lasted for about a decade, but it had lasting ramifications on our national apple diversity. America used to have a thriving cider industry, sporting a range of almost twenty-thousand apple varieties. Prohibition resulted in the destruction of thousands of orchards and most of these varieties perished. Today in a grocery store you will typically only find about four or five types of apples, none of which are great cider-making apples.

America has seen a large resurgent interest in the cider business, with hundreds of new cider producers opening all across the nation. The public has seen a renewed taste for the drink, and with it has come the quest for new apple varieties. This is readily apparent when you visit a European pub. The quality of taste in European ciders greatly exceeds those of America. It's not even a close competition. More efforts need to be made to import and proliferate rare apple varieties to restore the craft.

It is difficult to imagine an opportunity quite like this one. A dead industry is almost never revived, but here we are in 2020, and Americans are drinking ciders again and listening to vinyl records. In this case, the government was almost entirely responsible for the destruction of the cider industry and it's near hundred-year road to recovery. It only took a decade to ruin it, let's see what a decade of supporting it could do. Imagine the profit opportunities of American based cider exports. We have the opportunity to make that happen. Make American Apples Great Again.

How do you like them apples? Democrats can take the lead on this issue and will find a great deal of rural support for it. Cider facilities are typically localized and operated as small businesses. They employ locals and many of them become centers for socialization. They share an intimate relationship with their orchard vendors and distributors. These are excellent microcosms for the kind of grassroots support that Democrats need to win in rural communities.

I want to see American ciders stand proudly on the shelves of foreign pubs, but they're not going to thrive until we get them some better apples.

Only all of us working together can prevent forest fires!

In the year 2020, there were somewhere around 52,000 wildfires across the United States, causing the destruction of almost 9 million acres of forests. In just the state of California alone this amounted to around $10 billion in damage. With human intervention, we can regrow something akin to a forest within about a decade or so and we've even become somewhat adept at simulating old growth. This is a very labor-intensive process that realistically takes decades. At the rate of millions of acres per year lost to fire we're not going to have forests anymore if this continues unabated. The number and severity of fires should be going down if we were strategically addressing this problem. Climate change is giving us a run for our money, but much of it is just human ignorance.

One of the largest fires in the history of California was ignited by a "gender-reveal party" gone horribly wrong. Millions of acres of irreparable damage and billions of dollars wasted just so we could find out the gender of a couple's baby with a smoke laced incendiary device. Smokey the Bear ought to come kick their ass. We cannot tolerate these sorts of accidents and mishaps. If it only takes a single couple to set off a million-acre fire, we have a serious problem.

The technology and the knowledge exists. This is not a problem with unknown solutions. This is not a tragedy that couldn't be predicted or prevented. We have entire agencies devoted to this. They just don't have the manpower or the funding to do everything that needs to be done.

Something as important as the oxygen we breathe ought to be taken seriously. The preservation of America's beautiful forests needs a higher priority.

The National Forest Service does the best it can under the circumstances. Over half of their budget is devoted to fighting and preventing fires. This has been a huge expansion in costs over the past few decades. Congress has recently given it a minor increase in funds, but it's not sufficient to cover our actual needs.

I recommend that we separate the fire fighting responsibility out of the purview of the Forest Service. Let them spend that money on conservation, education outreach, and fire prevention instead. Establish a separate agency devoted exclusively to the rapid deployment of fire fighting services. Instead of having to pull firefighters away from other states and rely on the help of inmate labor to fight these fires, we should have federal support at the ready. We have it for so many other reasons. There is much preparation for helping people after a disaster has occurred, but what about stopping the disaster as it's occurring to prevent it from getting worse? We've been able to land a man on the moon for fifty years, why can't we stop a forest fire in our own backyard?

Part of it is the lackluster education about forestry in schools. There is some discussion about it, a few field trips even. Some secondary students even get some fire training. Otherwise, if you're not a Boy Scout you don't hear much about forestry. Smokey the Bear is not turning the heads that he used to. I would like to see more education programs take a proactive approach to environmental science.

We need more programs that get young people involved with conservation, fire fighting, trail building, and forest maintenance. They could be out there taking in the fresh air, getting physical activity, and enjoying the mental health benefits of a walk in the woods, while also learning, building, and preparing our forests to avoid fires. This could make them better stewards of the land, teach them to avoid stupidity with fire, and also how to safeguard their property from potential hazards. AP classes are great and all, but I would much rather see a practical framework with kids learning how to drive better, protect the woods, and hammer a nail. There ought to be honors classes for skilled labor to encourage more kids to take those courses. I genuinely believe that the things that I learned in extracurricular programs like Scouting were far more impactful and useful to me and to society than most of the things that I learned at school.

Americans in *red* parts of the states would actually love to hear that. They want to see young people out there physically interacting with the environment and doing things. They value their hunting and fishing lands and want to see those protected. They want the condition of their property to be maintained. They can also easily understand why we cannot afford to spend billions of dollars on property damage every year due to fires. This is why almost every municipality in the country has its own firefighting agency, some of them even serving as volunteers. The interest is there if you approach it the right way.

The difficult part is convincing people to fund fire fighting measures at the federal level. If the fire isn't happening in their state, they don't want to pay for it. Who could forget the time that Louisiana governor Bobby Jindal went on a tirade about the funding of volcano monitoring, calling it wasteful. The governor of Washington was quick to fire back that they gladly fund hurricane relief efforts in the state of Louisiana on an almost annual basis. If you live somewhere with tornados you want tornado sirens. If you live somewhere with active volcanoes you want someone monitoring them. If you live on a fault line you want to monitor seismic activity. If you live on the Atlantic or in Gulf States you have to be ready for hurricanes. If you live in the Midwest or the Great Lakes, you have to be ready for heavy snowfall. It's easy to say that these places should each pay their own way towards managing their weather crises, but that's inherently unpatriotic. When a hurricane strikes New Orleans, Bobby Jindal expects FEMA to be there. It's only fair that they return the favor when California is on fire. America's strength comes from our unity and our ability to help one another during our hour of need. We cover you so that you will cover us in return and we can all get back on our feet sooner after a crisis.

We sometimes forget that the most obvious things need to be repeatedly enforced. Common knowledge only becomes common if it is talked about and committed to in perpetuity. As a teacher, I often have to step back and give consideration to how I present a topic. My students genuinely do not know certain things, because they have never been taught certain things. This is no fault of their own. This is the very purpose of education. We cannot presume that the public knows, we just have to presume that they can learn. We don't have to be condescending about these things or insult their intellectual capabilities. Just present the information regularly and repeatedly. If the governor doesn't understand the need to federally fund something, explain why we do. Discuss the budget and the consequences of inaction. Be transparent about it. Americans can make their own determinations.

Design the national fire brigade with this interstate misunderstanding in mind. Much like the All-Star League brings professional baseball players from teams across the nation, the fire force should include delegations and branches in all fifty states. This increases the likelihood of rapid response, and also encourages buy-in because now you're talking about jobs. It is easy for people in Dallas, a place with no forests, to ignore the problem. They send volunteers, but ultimately there is something about all that money going to an agency they have no ties to that rubs people the wrong way. However, if you throw a fire force office in every state, and you employ a hundred or so people, you get the public vested in the process. This would also help ease the burden on existing local fire resources. It can be costly, but when you need it, you will be glad it's there.

National Park at Allegheny National Forest.

While we are on the subject of strengthening public perception through inclusion, we should discuss areas of the nation that are federally deficient. It's difficult to get people to invest in a service that they do not have or use regularly. One way to do that is to locate a group of great federal jobs to places that could really benefit from them.

Democrats have been struggling to maintain Pennsylvania in recent elections and it is among the states most needed for victory in the Electoral College. This was once a safe state for Democrats, but they cannot sustain a winning coalition by putting all of their eggs in the Philadelphia and Pittsburgh metropolitan areas.

There are many areas of Pennsylvania that are still struggling due to the loss of formerly profitable coal mining and steel jobs. These rural areas are trending deeply red, and throwing some good-paying federal jobs their way could really go a long way for Democrats at the ballot box. The Allegheny National Forest covers a huge portion of Northwestern Pennsylvania and I believe establishing a National Park there could be of beneficence.

National Forests and National Parks have very different land use goals, and independent budgets. They tend to work closely together, and the average American doesn't know one from the other. I am not suggesting that we change the status of the entire forest. The goal is to keep the same level of National Forest presence there but to also bring in the National Park presence there. This would require the agencies to carve out a more scenic section of land for the park and devise an asset transfer plan.

This would promote greater tourism to the area, which could benefit local communities along the route from area population centers. It creates new job opportunities for the people of the local communities. The park will need new rangers and a visitors center to house them in. Roads will need to be built. Trails and campgrounds will need to be built or upgraded. Towns in the surrounding region will need to build accommodations. The money goes further out there, and the ripple effect of that additional investment would likely be far more valuable than the partial loss to the National Forest Service.

There are quite a number of places that could benefit from a National Park boom, but I selected this particular area for consideration because a large portion of it is already federal land. It is also strategic in nature. These counties went heavily for Trump, voting for him by margins in excess of 70%. If Democrats can take credit for some quality job creation and economic stimulus in the region, they could hopefully reduce those margins to help them win statewide races.

While urban support for Democrats is probably at an all-time high, we can see that Republicans are winning rural areas with equally huge margins. If Democrats want to start winning more races, they need to start bringing the message and the benefits out to these communities. They can do this by targeting micro population centers.

The town of Warren, PA would stand to benefit the most from a National Park in this location. It has a population of about 10,000, and the whole county has maybe 20,000 voters in it. These numbers do not attract just a whole lot of interest from campaigners, but they should and that is part of the problem. You don't have to convince all of them to vote for you, you only need about 4,000 more. From a percentage perspective it sounds challenging to do, but in reality, how difficult is it to reach out to the right people in a small town? A handful of grassroots organizers could easily knock on 4,000 additional doors. Money would also go much further there because it will always be less expensive to campaign in rural areas than it will in urban areas.

The current Democratic model for victory is nuclear. The blast radius is the center of the largest population centers, and it radiates outward into the surrounding areas. This creates a contraction and expansion effect to election victories, and it makes Democrats easy targets for the gerrymander as I expressed previously. I would propose a move towards a trickle inward effect. Democrats are barely hanging on to Erie County right now. If they can start to break down barriers in Warren and Crawford County, they will also see their margins in Erie start to increase. They don't have to actually win there, they just need to purple things out enough on the edges to solidify their exurban fringe. Republicans have used this to make inroads for years. They target the micro-population centers in rural communities and they besiege the major urban areas they surround. Their support pushes back into the suburbs that Democrats need to win.

Democrats need to plant an anchor in the desert. It may be expensive for just one county in Pennsylvania, but if you do it strategically it pushes back into your core and keeps you winning in the places that you have to. I could draw some easy circles on the map of the counties Democrats should be spending their campaign money on that they are not. They spent almost $51 million on Cal Cunningham's senate bid, just so he could fizzle out. Compare this to the race for House District 6 in PA between Michael Ferrence and Bradley Roae. Democrats spent about $20,000 on the race. Only about 25,000 people voted. What do you suppose the outcome might have been if Democrats had given even a quarter-million of that Super PAC money to Michael Ferrence? No one considered it a competitive race, but that's only because the Democrats weren't really competing. I understand the importance of winning back the Senate, but sometimes investing in the big candidate isn't helping the big candidate win. For a half-million dollars, Michael Ferrence could have held a major campaign rally every day for the entire election year, utilizing every small business in the county. There are thousands of small-town races all over America that Democrats could be winning if they put their money into it.

Picture for a moment how things could have gone very differently in North Carolina, sex scandal aside. For $51 million, Democrats could have spent $3.6 million in all 13 House districts in North Carolina, and still had another $3.6 million for Cal. Now you have 14 eggs in the basket, instead of 1. This money is going to go significantly further. It gets spent locally by people who know their neighborhoods better, and if each of them turns out another couple thousand voters, They probably could have put Cal over the top, better than Cal running a statewide campaign could do for himself. Instead of every single elected Democrat riding the coattails of the Presidential candidate, flip the script. Let the higher candidates get pushed into office, by the hands of the grassroots efforts the local candidates are making on behalf of the party. How do you think Stacey Abrams delivered Georgia for Biden? He wasn't pulling himself up, she was pushing him in.

A National Park would plant a big pretty solid seed in Northwestern Pennsylvania. The federal dollars go much further there than they do elsewhere. For the price of Cal's loss, Democrats could have quintupled the amount of funds spent on Barbara Bollier's campaign. They could have delivered that Senate seat in ruby-red Kansas. The beauty in that is that Republicans would also be scrambling for the defensive. When Democrats start putting their money on unexpected bets, it forces Republicans to withdraw their hand from their less confident races to protect their strongholds.

Look at the unexpected surprises over the last few election cycles. Picking up a Democratic senator in Alabama, Doug Jones. Winning the state of Georgia. If Republicans were scrambling to defend themselves in places like Nebraska, Oklahoma, or Kansas, they would have had fewer funds to spend on races like North Carolina. This might net a surprise win for a Democrat elsewhere, and simultaneously boost those key races just by getting the opponent off their back. Now I realize campaign funds are attributed to the candidate raising them, but I'm talking primarily about SuperPAC money being spent by the party as an entity or its affiliates. Use the party money to go on the offense by targeting micro-population centers.

Notice I have not had to discuss environmental issues to make this happen. I did not have to talk about global warming or regulations. I didn't even have to go into great detail about the merits of environmental conservation. I can frame these environmental issues as one of job creation or I can frame it as an issue of mitigating potentially expensive property damage and loss of use. Approaching someone and asking them if they care about saving the salmon in a state they've never been to, probably won't garner much support. You can present the same bill by telling them that taking no action would cause a catastrophic financial loss to the fishing industry. Then you can follow it up with how it will raise the prices of fish and meat at their local grocery store and lastly that it would allow foreign competitors to gain a larger market share, further exacerbating the U.S. trade imbalance. The end result is the same, you save the salmon. You just sold it better in the second proposition. Whether or not they should care about something is irrelevant, because almost everyone cares about money. As much as I wish people cared, I have to contend with a reality where they don't, and the Democrats need to get smart about presentation.

Bigger isn't Better: Corporate Reform

Bigger isn't Better: Corporate Reform

Ban the practice of golden parachutes.

Incentivize increased salary-based pay with tax offsets for wage increases.

SBA Loans for worker-owned enterprises.

Enforce antitrust laws and review mergers with higher scrutiny.

Reduce permitting, taxation, and regulation requirements for small businesses.

Change bankruptcy laws to protect employees.

Impose aggressive tax policies on offshore account safe havens.

Executive pay ceiling that caps relative to percent of lowest company wage earners.

Prioritize long term planning over short term capital gains.

Golden Parachutes

Thanks for all the memories, unfortunately the company is going out of business. We're laying everyone off and filing for bankruptcy. Unfortunately your pension could not be spared. Your insurance will soon expire. The company stock we gave you instead of real compensation is now worthless. This is not because your labor has changed. We purposefully mismanaged the company because it resulted in short-term gains for our shareholders. Don't worry we will go ahead and pay out the rest of those non-rollover vacation days you never got to use. The company was in such dire straits that we would only afford to pay each of our 100 executive vice presidents a $5 million bonus on the way out the door. I'm sure you'll understand.

This is the story of the modern business environment. Executives run a company into the ground only to escape on a golden parachute with a total disregard for the communities or employees who rely on the company for their livelihood. They practically reward themselves for their own failure. It's almost more profitable to get booted from your contract or destroy the company than it is to stay and do a good job. The rich truly live on a different planet from the rest of society. It's time to bring them back down to Earth, because working Americans have no time for bullshit.

Let me be the first to tell you what you already know. Executives are not necessary and American companies are top heavy with inflated millionaires. Everyone who has worked in a corporate environment knows what "vice president" means. They spend most of their day attending meetings that are purportedly very important, where they make up company policy that no one wants, isn't helpful, and doesn't involve input from the people who actually do work for a living. Then they'll pay one of their consultant buddies a few million dollars to canvass why the policy they made isn't working. It's these kinds of people that made Karl Marx contemplate a world where workers seized the means of production, and probably the reason why Marie Antionette lost her head. At natural law you reap what you sow. When people begin to realize someone else has been eating all their crops, they eventually do something about it.

As a person who has numerous graduate degrees, a heaping pile of diverse work experiences, and who once owned a corporation, I can tell you that there is absolutely nothing special about a corporate executive. Aside from the rare innovator, most executives have no direct involvement in the labor market of their industry. They have no idea what it is their employees actually do, they don't know the product or service their company provides, they just happened to be born rich, and were well connected to other rich people who got them jobs as executives.

A friend of mine climbed the ladder at a tech firm for years. Eventually he got promoted to an isolated contract within the company he was working for. He was the only person on the contract and worked at an offsite office, where he was serving as the in-house technical support for an entire skyscraper. After a few years things started getting ridiculous. After his last manager in the company left, they were never replaced. He was still getting paid, but he reported to no one. Many people would dream of the opportunity to be left alone in this matter, until they realize that it leaves little room for raises, bonuses, promotions, or opportunities to grow as a professional. The office building could have just hired him directly as their own technical support specialist, and would have only spent 1/4th of the cost of their contract with the company he worked for. In Texas, the employer would have very little recourse. The right-to-work legislation is a two way street, and Texas is not fond of anti-competition covenants.

He had been informing management of his intent to leave the company for almost a year, and they took absolutely no interest in hearing him out. He landed a job at another firm, and he put in his two-week notice. The CEO of his company, whom he had never met, talked to the CEO of the company he was leaving for in a desperate attempt to derail the changeover. The exchange was quite underhanded, with his current CEO essentially trash-talking about his technical competency and saying that he needed significant intervention from the company to do his job. After the call, the CEO of the company he was leaving to work for called to inform him of the conversation and suggested he set up a transition plan for them to smooth the waters. His current CEO called immediately afterward to ask him what it was he did at the company, because he didn't know. After making specific false comments about his technical abilities, the CEO had absolutely no idea what he did. He didn't even know about the nature of the contract. He just knew that he needed to try to retain him for the sake of the contract. They had absolutely no plan to replace him because the executive team was so ignorant that they didn't even know he worked there. My point to this story is that most executives are so far removed from the operations of the company that they are not competent enough to run it.

Executive is a position that they supposedly earned because they were "a visionary" and because they "worked hard" to reach that level. I have known a few of them in my time, and I probably have photos somewhere of them doing keg stands at my frat parties, because they were just like anybody else once. The only difference is that they had everything paid for their entire lives, and while you were busting your ass to make ends meet, they were able to grow their money on the market, not incur debt, and use their connections to get them everything they needed. If you've got it, use it. We all would if given the chance. That doesn't mean our society should cater to them by sanctioning their bad behavior with our government.

CEOs are currently compensated at a rate of almost 1000% or higher above the base level employee of the corporation they run. To put this into perspective, imagine you are a minimum wage worker making $1,200 a month. The CEO of your company is taking home $1,200,000 a month. What economic justification supports this? The claim is that they set the vision and direction for the company. They take responsibility (well kind of) for the company. They are supposed to act as a sort of balance between the company needs and those of the shareholders.

Let me present an alternative vision for you. My megacorporation sells hamburgers. My hamburger stand sells 100 burgers a day on a staff of 5 employees, each who make that $1,200 monthly amount. If the corporation got rid of its CEO, it could hire 1,200 additional workers at that same base-level amount. Alternatively, it could compensate each of its burger flippers $240,000 a month instead. People who are directly tied to the business activity itself. Alternatively, the company could pay 100 people $12,000 per month to come in, sell one burger and leave to go enjoy the rest of their lives. It's not entirely that simple or lucrative as my example, but the CEO compensation level is that ridiculous and it is actively harming the average American worker.

If the entire staff leaves the burger company, the CEO cannot single-handedly go in and make the 100 burgers. They don't even know how to do that. Workers of the past fought hard, sometimes violently for their rights and their compensation. They knew the power of the strike. If you aren't there to build it, they aren't there to run it. The wealthy elite of America have invested heavily in union-busting legislation precisely for this reason. Most base-level workers are so heavily dependent on their meager daily wages for survival that they won't take the risk to strike. Hence the very need to take the risk and unionize anyway. The base-level workers outnumber the holders of capital by thousands to one and they outvote them too. Until executive compensation is fair and reasonable, they should all refuse to work. It's not Communism, it's saying no to economic hubris. It doesn't make any financial sense to compensate an executive at that level of disparity.

If I was on the Board of Directors and I wanted to maximize profits and value to shareholders, I would ditch the entire executive team and just promote a few mid-level managers from within. They are not even 1/8th as expensive, and they would probably do a better job because they know what's going on at the ground floor. Paying one person 1000% more ought to be considered a breach of fiduciary duty because it's unbelievably wasteful.

This brings us back to our original insult to injury. If your company executives are going to get millions of dollars in handouts on the way out the door, then your company obviously isn't hurting that badly. There should be no bankruptcy protections for companies that pay out golden parachutes. You don't get to lay everyone off, cancel their benefits, and walk away with millions of dollars and a get-out-of-the-mud free card. Those millions of dollars should go into sustaining the operations of the company and executive compensation should be the first thing slashed in a downturn. Employees should not be losing everything, while executives are getting a bonus. When the ship is sinking an honorable captain is the last one off the boat. Get an executive that goes down with the ship trying to steer it to safety, not the asshole in first-class filling the life-boats half full for their convenience.

This strikes fear in the hearts of a board of directors, because if there was no executive team who would attend all of those meetings? Your suspicions about meetings have been correct for decades. Most meetings are not discussion-oriented. They are directive in nature. These kinds of meetings could have been an email. Most meetings are just scheduled, and there is no need for them to happen at all because they have no bearing on the reality of the work environment. The accountants will count the money. Contracts specialists will sign contracts. Human resources will pay the payroll taxes. Productions will build it. Why have the middleman coordinating it all, when all they do is relay directives from the board?

I theorize that I could design a computer program to automate every function of the executive. The board could just type their demands into a computer, and an artificial intelligence could rephrase it into barely comprehensible jargon that makes the demand sound reasonable and valuable. Then it could email the message out to all of the department managers, who actually lead their teams. This would free up countless hours wasted in meetings that don't need to happen and probably achieve the same results for a fraction of the cost. I doubt most people would even notice their CEO was a robot.

This is not to say that all CEOs are worthless. There are plenty of good ones out there doing great work at an honest and fair compensation level. Banning golden parachutes causes no harm to CEOs of merit and integrity. If the justification for keeping them is that qualified executives would otherwise quit doing the job, you haven't met Americans. There's someone highly qualified in every company eager to take their place if they leave, parachute or not.

Incentive for Salary Pay

If companies paid employees a fair and honest wage to compensate them for their true human value, we would hardly need the assistance of the government at all in matters of public welfare. The race to the bottom for wages is both morally bankrupt and fiscally irresponsible. A multitude of companies have staked their wealth upon the foundation that if they paid higher wages, they would lose more profits. This shortsightedness fails to see the totality of the circumstances. When your employees are doing well, your product or service will also do well. If your consumer base is all being chronically undervalued, they have less money to put back into your company. You essentially drain your own bank by hoarding all the money upfront without giving it a chance to multiply its value in the open market first.

The era of hourly wage labor has run its course. When the function of jobs involved how quickly a worker could produce the most amount of a product, compensating time was a sensible means of consistency in payment.

More productive workers could be compensated more per hour because they were making more. These jobs were not really thought of with any sense of permanence. People worked the time that they wanted or needed to, and either moved up, moved on, or died.

In modern times people expect that their job will meet certain requirements. They desire to be compensated for the position that they fulfill rather than the time that they spend there. The forty-hour work week has seen about a century of idealized popularity. The system of benefits has evolved almost entirely around it. The purpose of time-based compensation has no meaning in a system where everyone is working forty hours. It only matters for purposes of overtime wages, which tend to be as predictable as they are inconsistent. It makes it very difficult for an hourly worker to accurately assess their true annual earnings and creates a host of financial dilemmas for the average American.

Salary-based pay is supposed to be the answer. Workers are compensated for the job itself rather than the time it takes to do it. Unfortunately, this can lead to wide variations in job responsibilities, where salary employees become perpetually on the clock. Nations such as France have fiercely protected a worker's personal time through legislation. France is still among the top ten economic superpowers in the world, but their workers are able to enjoy months of vacation, and a definitive end to their workdays. Who is really winning here?

There were weeks at Caterpillar I was working for eighty hours. I enjoyed it because I wanted the overtime checks, however, I couldn't help but think of the incredibly detrimental impact this had on my coworkers who had fewer options and never got to see their families. As a result of my experience there I have come to be fiercely protective of my personal time as well.

What these two systems have led to is the illusion of productivity. We become experts at appearing to be busy at our jobs when often we are not. I was once working the night shift unpacking trucks and stocking shelves at Target. It was there that I came to realize the fallacy of the hourly wage. Some nights we could clear three trucks at six thousand pieces in a period of eight hours. Other nights we could clear one truck with two thousand pieces.

Do you suppose that it took us a third of the time it took to unload the three? Not at all. It still took eight hours. That's because everyone relied on eight hours for their paycheck each day. Some days you might break a sweat trying to unload as much as you could in time. Other days you would take your sweet time carefully positioning each box of cereal on the shelf. Perhaps one every few minutes just to kill the time.

One of my coworkers was Chinese. He had no understanding or patience for our lack of efficiency and work ethic. He would stock his section as fast as he could, then clock out and go to his shelf-stocking job somewhere else. He would only get paid for the few hours he worked while the rest of us were getting eight hours standing still. Americans are not collectively as stupid as our employers believe we are. They can make all the efficiency quotas they want, but somehow they're still always paying out forty hours a week. This system isn't helping anyone and it doesn't value our humanity.

If they had paid us the same amount on salary, our productivity would have skyrocketed. We all would have been like the Chinese man, in and out in three hours. The job is completed. The workers are compensated. Who gives a shit what they do with the remaining five hours of their day? It would free up more time to engage in other economic opportunities. Time to enjoy life. Time to invest in creative pursuits and education. Time to spend with family and friends. Holding a worker hostage for their time when their job is based on task completion is as inhumane as it is unproductive.

The same problem is true of salary positions as well. Non-customer facing jobs are often task-based in nature and could be completed in a fraction of the time allotted by the forty-hour work week. Knowing that the reward for completing your tasks early is the assignment of more tasks, only encourages workers to be unproductive. That report magically took eight hours to complete. That set of procedures took eight hours. That memorandum was challenging. It took eight hours. When you require salaried employees to be in a place and be available for a period of time, they will fill that time so that they only barely complete their work tasks within it. It reduces the anxiety of looking busy and it avoids being *rewarded* with extra work. What reason do employees have to be more productive? If your first thought was promotions and bonuses, please hear the chorus of laughter in the background from all the Americans who have been promised that and never saw it delivered.

These problems create a hostile and adversarial relationship between employers and employees that need not exist. They come up with production quotas, monitoring systems, evaluations, performance reviews. They devise a punitive system to try to get workers to fill their time with tasks, even though the tasks they are contacted to fulfill do not require it. What we deem as quality performance is actually overperformance. They are not completing their job as required. They are filling the time with the job above and beyond what is required or even useful.

During the Covid pandemic, all I have heard about is how eager everyone is to resume business as usual. I frankly hope that they don't. I hope that this has given us all pause to see that we can be just as productive at our jobs without Father Time watching us work. In fact, I found that I could do my job better in the absence of the constant disruptions of false productivity. At one point I spent a week in a cabin in Tennessee. I still did my job, even as I stood at the base of a waterfall. With my reclaimed time, I was able to write three books, produce an album, and lose thirty lbs in the span of about 9 months. My job was still done well and I had a record year of productivity for my personal life. When not burdened by frivolity, new economic opportunities become available, and that is a benefit to all of society.

The first step towards getting our nation on the road to better compensation practices is to promote salary wages. Pay for the job, not for the time. The focus of the conversation is often on how we can increase the minimum wage if you're a Democrat, and how you can reduce business taxes if you're a Republican. Both of these can actually be done simultaneously.

I propose a dollar-per-dollar business tax decrease for the quantity of salaried wages above a certain value. That value would be set above the rate at which a citizen would require public assistance. A maximum deduction would apply to prevent companies from using it all on a handful of executive employees (because God knows they would!). Businesses can either do the right thing and pay a fair wage, or they can pay taxes so the government can do it for them. It costs them nothing additional from what they currently pay now, but incentivizes them to pay employees more.

Republicans and Democrats both get what they want and society is better off for it. The government would reclaim the lost revenue in the form of additional income taxes and cost savings. It's a win for all.

SBA Loans for worker-owned enterprises

Worker-owned enterprises are a great solution to most problems involving corporate greed. Corporate environments like to speak about a family or team-like atmosphere that doesn't really exist. What incentive do you have to be innovative at your job? When the company is doing well are you really doing well? Does your family really treat you that way?

Donald Trump stood before America and promised that his deep business tax cuts would trickle down into Americans' pockets. The promise was that if businesses paid less taxes they could pay their workers more. They spent it on stock buybacks and executive bonuses.

I recall a company meeting to discuss the wonderful news about how the stock buybacks would make the company stronger and that it would help us retain our jobs. We asked for clarity on when we would see a raise on our checks. The answer was never. It was a magic trick. Trump and his friends looted the public and got praised for it.

The reality is that at the end of the day when the balance of power is as uneven as it is in a megacorporation, executives can't resist the temptation to help themselves to the company coffers. It's always going to be a system that takes instead of a system that shares. There is a reason why the stock market can be doing well, but the public at large is still suffering. It's a crisis of ownership imbalance that has given rise to this unfortunate class of American aristocrats.

In a worker-owned cooperative system, the members of the company are on equitable terms. They all share an ownership interest in the cooperative, and they are all fully invested in the outcome. The leadership of the cooperative is selected among members. You won't see them voting for 1000% wage disparities or spending their tax relief funds on lavish bonuses. When you apply democracy to business decision making, you get a better outcome.

These workers know their products and services. They are passionate about them. The success of the company is their success. These are strong companies that America desperately needs more of.

The next time a company packs up and leaves town, rather than boarding it up and sending it into a downward economic spiral, workers should view this as an opportunity to recapture ownership of their community. Unfortunately, when half the town loses their job there isn't much that a bank will invest in. The capital dries out and any possibility of saving the town goes under with it.

The Small Business Administration should extend grants or loans to these communities in an effort to keep workers in the community through the establishment of worker-owned cooperatives. Rather than bailing out the giant corporation as it is abandoning the town or going under, we could invest in establishing a stronger community-oriented set of businesses, owned by the members of the community. The initial investment would carry some burden of risk, but ultimately the return on investment would be much greater if we intervened in a community before it collapsed, instead of spending decades trying to revive it when the spark has gone out.

Corporate and Wall Street bailouts do not sit well with the American people, even when they are successful. The reason why Democrats are trending so poorly in small towns right now is because they never got a Mainstreet bailout. While the rich have recovered spectacularly from the Great Recession, regular people are still barely hanging on. Many do not believe they will ever recover their retirement losses. They are worried about paying their student loans. They are worried they may never make enough money to buy a house. Now they are getting shut down by the pandemic. Supporting the formation of worker-owned cooperatives is an insurance policy for the middle class and it's time that we start investing in them.

Mergers & Trustbusters

How big is too big? Corporations have been engaging in mergers and takeovers for a few decades now, conglomerating into ever-expanding networks. There is something close to thirty American companies with earnings that could rank it ahead of some nations' entire GDP. In this era, they are primarily technology companies like Google, Facebook, and Amazon.

The Federal Trade Commission has finally taken an interest in these companies after years of either ignoring them or failing to understand them. This comes on the heels of perhaps the most astonishing inquisition in modern history where Congress brought in tech giants like Mark Zuckerberg and asked them how they needed to be regulated. He surprisingly came to their aid making pointed suggestions for how they could improve their legislation. Not only did he make them look like the idiots they were, but he also helped them write laws that were actively against his interest.

The average age of Congress is significantly older than people who know how the internet works. It was frankly not at all surprising that Hillary Clinton had a server scandal. I was actually just impressed that a Senator knew how to check their own email. It was even more disappointing to see President Trump use Twitter the same way a 13-year-old Millennial once used Xanga. If that joke is lost on you, then you shouldn't be tweeting either. This is a great argument for term-limits, but also somewhat terrifying to think that these people run a tech economy without knowing what that means.

They finally started to pay attention to technology acquisitions, and now they are concerned about the sudden lack of competition. I would argue that our current antitrust laws are not even adaptable to these types of companies. They were designed during a time where commodity and process control was king. The modern tech company does not provide commodities or processes, but rather a hosting platform and a user base.

This to me is the equivalent of a digital building. The website rather than being a commodity is a structural entity. Facebook is not a thing, it's a place. They're just a property management company. At best you can treat them like an advertising firm. It's not even an essential commodity. What Congress doesn't realize is how quickly and easily consumer tastes can change. Facebook is huge today, but ten years ago it was Myspace, and before that it was Xanga, and before that it was LiveJournal. Is there no irony in the President tweeting on a different social media platform about how Facebook is monopolistic?

We went through a similar transformation with music. First, it was Apple that purportedly monopolized the industry with Itunes. Then Spotify came along and a ton of customers made the switch because it offered a better platform. This makes internet services distinctly different from a commodity like oil. There's no difference in the end product between Exxon-Mobil, Shell, or BP. They compete on other fronts. Standard Oil was different because it controlled every avenue of the production process, so it could effectively deny others from gaining access to raw materials because it owned all of them. You can't do that with the internet.

The internet is a public utility. Anyone is free to create a new platform, or switch between platforms, just the same as they might walk into a Wal-Mart, a Target, and a local coffee shop all in the same day. Where tech companies have got themselves into trouble are some of the services they're offering. Netflix, Prime, and Hulu all have original series they're producing now. Does that open the gates to monopoly? AmazonBasics is producing essential products at a cut-rate price. Are they still a retail platform, or are they the producer? No one would argue against the right of a store to offer a store brand, or for a retailer to diversify its product offerings. It's not inherently monopolistic. It's just a giant corporation like all the physical brick-and-mortar ones.

When you start to look at Amazon's warehousing and delivery services it starts to look a bit more problematic, but it hasn't changed anything. We still get packages from UPS and FedEx and I don't hear them hurting for profits or market share in an ever-expanding market.

What about Google? They dominate the personal email industry. They dominate the search engines. They offer the only viable alternative to Microsoft's Office Suite. Google Fiber. They have Google Wallet, Google Classroom, a popular cell phone line, Google just about anything you could imagine. Nest thermostats and other home electronics. These things are not necessarily monopolistic individually. It's just like any other huge megacorporation. If Google were to start buying up rare Earth mineral mines and excluding their competitors, then we could call it a monopoly in the traditional sense. Otherwise, our only option is to break up the services that

Google offers, but this becomes problematic under existing law to prove necessary in court.

It's difficult to measure comparisons between technological products. There are easy counter-arguments to existing monopolistic claims. We shouldn't punish companies for innovation and success. Some products are just objectively better. We use these products because they offer a better interface or service not because we lack alternatives. If we bust them up into separate entities they would fail to function as a cohesive unit. They would lose the platform integration that has become an essential part of their appeal. Indeed many people would agree the internet has actually improved with less competition.

Nobody drives a Studabaker or a Pontiac anymore. Is it because their competitors ate them or because they failed to innovate and took the business in a direction the consumer didn't want to follow? It's difficult to parse out an insidious merger, from a legitimate acquisition. Tech companies can easily claim that their market share is driven by consumer preference and to date they can usually find at least one alternative competitor that still has a fighting share of the market.

Nonetheless, who can compete with these companies? Given their financial power, they can afford to innovate and purchase new utilities and platforms in ways that no other companies can. They can retain the best people. The tech company's monopoly does not rest in its control of physical resources as much as it rests in its control over capital and retention of customers.

Their ability to exploit tax loopholes and the ease at which they can shift assets to make money disappear makes tech companies very difficult to reign in. I can easily tax a manufacturer because I can always find the factory and it's not easily relocated. Internet-based companies are different. When everything you own and sell is online you can shift your workforce and your base of operations anywhere in the world in a matter of days.

If Congress wants to get serious about opening up the competition, they have to change the way that they tax these entities. You cannot tax a tech company the same as you tax another business entity. The problem is that these companies are so large and so global that even talking about taxes has led to threats of international trade wars. You have to strike a unilateral international agreement among the economic superpowers and you have to do it quickly. The slow deliberation of taxation regulation gives these companies plenty of time to change everything about how they operate to avoid paying it. You cannot fault them for this though, they're doing what any sensible business would do and they're complying with the laws. It is more the fault of Congress for its inability to be decisive and deliberative.

They are hardly the first to do this. The business world has been inventing new business entities for decades to circumvent taxes. An entire industry has been built around tax avoidance. It's not even that difficult. There are so many deductions and write-offs out there that you can almost always make it look like you're running in the red. That's how Amazon has done it.

Here we are then. We have companies that are purportedly too big to fail, too big to compete against, and too big to tax. Most corporate mergers and buyouts have had detrimental impacts on consumers, causing prices to increase, so we know they're not helpful to the public at large. We see that they rarely result in new growth and do not result in increased employment opportunities. Failing companies often merge into one another in the hopes that two wrongs will make it a right and it almost never does. When one of these megacorporations finally does go under the financial loss ripples across the entire economy to such an extent that it can cause a global recession. Then we bail them out because we want to restore the jobs and economic activity lost.

The megacorporation thus becomes immune to bad decision making. They can make unlimited terrible shortsighted business decisions and still emerge victorious. It is not uncommon for corporations to create a business entity just for the purpose of dumping their bad decisions into it. They put all their garbage into a pile and separate it from the parent company. Then they light the match and let it burn. The bankruptcy fairy swoops in to save the day and all is forgiven. When you look at the totality of law, it almost seems like the regulations actually encourage and enable monopolies more than they prevent them.

Antitrust laws are thus slippery. If you follow the paper trail, you begin to realize that every major corporation in the world now owns all the other major corporations in the world. When you break up one, it just pops up somewhere else. We cannot expect the Teddy Roosevelt tactics to work in 2020 because the nature of business around the globe has fundamentally changed. We have too many eggs in one global basket. While there is risk distribution value to having large and diverse companies, at the point that you have integrated every business with every other business in the world, you lose the effect. Every failed business decision then hurts all businesses globally to some degree. It's not distributive if it is universal. Individual market crashes should not impact the entire global economy. That's not beneficial to anyone.

The first step to solving these problems is to block the mergers that create these megacorporations in the first place. If you only look at the profits of the companies in question in the merger, you have no true assessment of value, because it's so easy to hide money. Changes to anti-trust laws need to assess a dollar amount of all assets involved in the merger or acquisition deal irrespective of their liquidity. If the amount in question is above a certain threshold, it should automatically trigger a denial under antitrust. That way legitimate mergers can still continue, but the truly damaging ones are automatically stopped. It should not be discretionary in nature, but rather mandatory and automatic. This would prevent the variation in enforcement that can be observed between Presidents.

The local credit union buying out another small bank in town doesn't trigger a problem, but when a company like AT&T buys Time Warner that law would automatically block the merger. Such a law should also address hostile takeovers through stock purchase and treat them as a merger under the same company asset value terms. This should not be based on the stock purchase value, but rather the entirety of the company asset value because that is effectively what the participants of the takeover are gaining access to.

The second step is to stop bailing out megacorporations when they fail. No special tax treatment. No bailout packages. No special interest insurance deals. No limitless bankruptcy protections. It's going to hurt, but when this happens we are just going to have to rip the bandaid off. The losses will be devastating, but temporary. Rather than spending billions of dollars propping up a failed megacorporation, the government should bail out the everyday citizen who worked for that company. Provide workers with the capital to purchase or retain company assets for themselves. This allows the everyday citizen to keep their job and also provide them ownership opportunities not otherwise available to them. It punishes the short-sighted decision making of the executive team and the shareholders. This is preferable to our current system of using the working man's money to bail out the company he hates working for. Imagine getting your position cut, but finding out your tax dollars went to the company to keep it afloat. Bailout the people who got screwed over, not the people doing the screwing.

In summation, tax the existing monopolies and do so in a way that is globally applicable, instantaneous, and equitable. Block large mergers and buy-outs from occurring to prevent monopolistic businesses from forming in the first place. Let the megacorporations fail when they fail without government support.

Reducing Barriers for Small Business

It's not just the monopolistic competition stifling small business growth in this country. There are endless barriers to entry that reduce the potential and viability of small business. It is not all a matter of federal policy. Taxation does contribute to these problems, but local regulations can be just as damaging.

When a megacorporation goes to the bank, the bank gives them what they ask for. They get the premium low interest rates. They get extraordinary term lengths. They can have multiple loans going at once. Their access to capital is easy because there is confidence in their ability to back it up through assets. With insurance, neither the bank nor the business becomes truly responsible for repayment and they can always trash the insolvent loans into a shell corporation.

When you and I go into a bank as a small business, the bank gives us the rundown. Your personal credit is tied to the note. Your personal assets are tied to the note. If your loan becomes insolvent it's going to ruin your credit. They will come for everything you own to repay it. They also never approve the amount that you really want or need. They're going to give you a way higher interest rate. It's nothing personal, they just know you're a higher risk client.

The Small Business Administration can improve access to capital by guaranteeing a certain amount of high-risk lending for small businesses. The Federal Housing Administration does this with mortgages to incentivize lending to the everyday consumer. We could do the same thing for the everyday consumer's business. Then if we were really smart we could combine the two in the form of construction and renovation loans for hybrid residential and business infrastructure.

With limited access to capital, the small business then finds itself with a whole host of regulations and permits that it must comply with and obtain in order to operate. The amount is often the same regardless of the size of the entity. That $1,000 bond to the Railroad Commissioner might be peanuts to a large transporter, but for the independent contractor that's a huge upfront cost. For the average American, that amount represents close to a month's rent. The average megacorporation could lose $1,000 a day and not even notice. They should not be billed the same way or subjected to the same permitting requirements.

In order to start a business, it is not enough that you obtain the capital to purchase the equipment. You have to also gather enough capital to pay the government their startup fees. The cost of incorporating. Required employment posters. State tax ID number filing. Secretary of State filings. For our business, you had DOT permits for every state you operated in and the Federal Government. License and registration fees. A process server company to receive lawsuits on your behalf. Special stickers for the trucks with all your licensing information on it. Railroad Commissioner bonds. A tax filing entity. It costs thousands of dollars before you even get to the actual nature of the business.

Once you do finally obtain the permits to open and operate, there is a whole other set of challenges with the location of the business itself. Local regulations require square footage minimums. They require certain appearances to be maintained. They require parking minimums. They restrict your ability to engage in commercial activity at your home. There may be some compelling reasons for these, but most of them are excessive.

When I started my business, we ran it out of a car and conducted business meetings at the gas station Burger King. The amount of unnecessary bullshit required to obtain a physical location was so burdensome that we just got a P.O. Box and called it a day. There is nothing stupider than having to hold shareholder meetings between yourself, but you can't accept the risk of not incorporating because no ordinary person could subject themselves to liability of that magnitude.

All of this could be avoided through good sense governance. If your initial capital investment is less than a certain amount, the fees should be waived. Knowing that the difference between a closely held corporation and DBA is just you talking to yourself at a Burger King once a month, maybe we should just go ahead and extend the same privileges afforded to corporations to the DBA without the red tape.

I understand that we do not want people haphazardly turning their front lawn into a toxic waste dump, but I think we can draw reasonable delineations between using your own home for periodic business use and using it for continuous customer or equipment interaction. If I can operate my business safely out of a storage shed, maybe the square footage minimum could be waived. You can reduce barriers to entry while still maintaining public safety.

Let's say you are successful. You get all the permits. You open the business at a location. You've managed to overcome all the initial barriers to success, the taxes become the next thing trying to ruin you. While the megacorporation has an army of accountants hiding its money and finding every possible reimbursement, deduction, or credit available, most small business owners are lucky to have Turbotax on their side. From a percentage basis, small businesses always end up paying more.

Operating a one or two-man operation is exhausting. You are always on 24/7 trying to make your business happen. When you finally start to do well you want to hire employees. You hire your first employee. Now you have to obtain a whole new set of licenses and permits for them too. You have to pay for background checks, drug tests, citizenship data, whatever it may be.

Then you suddenly have new taxes.

You pay into state unemployment networks for every state of residence your employee lives in or works in. You pay a payroll tax to both the state(s) and the federal government. This has entirely separate filing entities and forms that are separate from your regular business taxes. The payroll tax also contains hidden costs that employees never see. Your employer actually has to pay a matching contribution to the government. While you have the opportunity to achieve some benefit from that contribution, the company gains absolutely nothing. The 7% tax to nowhere.

The ultimate impact of this is that the payroll tax actively disincentivizes hiring. Knowing that labor comes with all the extra work and the payments to nowhere, I have to think really hard about hiring the next employee. This goes hand in hand with my previous assessment of why taxation on income is detrimental.

I posit that if the government eliminated the payroll tax, companies would initiate enough additional hiring to fully offset the amount currently earned from the company portion of the payroll tax in the form of individual income taxes. This would primarily benefit small businesses. Megacorporations find plenty of creative tax loopholes to offset their payroll taxes as it is. Small businesses cannot afford such luxuries. I calculated this out for my business and determined it would have resulted in about a 15% decrease in my operating costs and would have allowed me to hire at least one additional employee. Imagine the benefits of every business in your town being able to hire one more person.

Business owners understand why we have taxes and regulations. We just want taxes and regulations that make sense. We want policies that incentivize us to do the right things, not policies that stand as barriers to entry. Nothing in government today should be accepted as it is. We need to reevaluate and question everything under a new lens. Who does it help? Who does it harm? What would change if we got rid of it? How fast could we bring it back if it turned out we did need it? Right now it seems that most of the policies designed to help people are actually harming them in other unintended ways. Let's reexamine those and come up with something that makes sense to all the stakeholders.

Chapter 69 Bankruptcy

When a company files for Chapter 11 it gets the opportunity to continue operating while it restructures its debts. It sounds great in theory. A struggling company in a recessionary state can get itself back on stable footing. Look deeper and you have to ask yourself why a company can't resettle its own debts without going to a court of law. Most large companies and creditors have negotiators and legal staff. They can easily forge an agreement on debt restructuring without a court's assistance. They could reach a mediated settlement agreement before even filing for bankruptcy. They could go to arbitration even. Bankruptcy for businesses isn't about debts. It's about expenses. Not just any expenses. It's about labor expenses.

Your workers have unionized and dragged you through the mud, asking for things like a living wage, healthcare, and time off with their families. How will you ever pay your CEO's golf tab? It's a real predicament. You sign the union agreement to get them off your back. Then you turn right around and file Chapter 11. Now I can lay off all those workers, suspend any collective bargaining agreements that I made, and use it as an excuse for why they shouldn't ask for more in the future. Then it's back to the 9-iron while the employees are in the doghouse.

Rather than getting rid of Chapter 11 in its entirety, I advocate for rewriting it to provide more favorable conditions for employees. When times were tough in my company, I personally went out and got a new job, just so I could continue to pay my employees. When we finally decided it wasn't worth it to continue, I paid off the company debt from my personal accounts. Today's company executives have no moral standards and bankruptcy law reflects that indecency. Companies should not be allowed to dismantle their union contracts in Chapter 11.

When creditors and corporations enter bankruptcy court they are essentially demanding that the public fix their problems for them. In most civil litigation the public has a vested interest in pursuing an intervention. The outcomes are such that it deters improper business practices, and we deem that to be a constructive means of resolving disputes where compensation is owed. What does the public get out of corporate bankruptcy? The answer is not a damn thing. The accomplishments of bankruptcy court can be achieved just as easily outside of court, and the only winners are the people who made the bad decisions leading to the debt in the first place.

Chapter 7 bankruptcy is a bit dicier. It results in the immediate liquidation of company assets to satisfy the creditors. Here is my problem with that. The creditor assumes almost no burden of risk. The government backs almost every loan they make on the public dime. Then they get to recover almost all of their losses while the people who work for the bankrupt company get the shaft. Their only remedy is to file for unemployment, a difficult and temporary solution.

I would like to propose an alternative to Chapter 7 bankruptcy, which I like to call Chapter 69 bankruptcy. Look who is getting fucked now! In my bankruptcy court, if you want the public to fix this problem, you have to give the public something in return. The forfeiting company will be recapitalized at the current share value of the company to compensate for the debt left unpaid. However, the stock will not be solely turned over to the creditor. It will instead be reallocated in equal shares with a one-third interest to the creditor, one-third interest to the current public shareholders, and one-third to the employees of the company.

This encourages all interested parties to work towards a common goal and puts them on an equitable footing. Something they should have done or could have done without the government getting involved. While public shareholders almost always pursue terrible business decisions to maximize their short-term gains, there is a strong incentive among shareholding employees and the creditors to make long-term strategic changes to restore profitability and reasonable share value. I haven't completely shut out the public shareholder though, they still keep some ownership interest and will hopefully be able to resurrect some of that value they would have completely lost in Chapter 7. Additionally, the court should appoint the first term of directors for the new company board, selecting candidates of choices from each group in equal proportions.

The creditor will still retain enough of an interest in the company that they can liquidate assets to recapitulate their loss, but they will have to do so quite slowly and in balance with the interest of the other shareholders. They are also free to sell their shares and cut their losses. They can also opt to purchase shares at market price from the other groups if there are willing sellers. If it obtains a majority share in the company, it can dissolve the company assets without the Court's help. Creditors will thus be incentivized to exercise greater care in decision making and will be forced to assume a portion of the loss that is their own making, rather than the nation or the community fitting the bill.

No more cut and run bankruptcies. Consideration for the livelihood of the participants involved should be the top priority. No worker should show up one day to find a chain locked factory door, without at least getting the opportunity to make a collective offer to purchase the assets there within at a fair and preferential cost. That is really the whole idea behind bankruptcy reform. When a corporation goes under and fractures, the government should attempt where possible to turn over control of the means of production to the employees of each fractured entity. Rather than shutting down a thousand stores across the nation, the government has a vested interest in empowering those employees to actualize self-destiny with the company assets. Divide the debt among each entity in equitable proportion and restructure it into a thousand individual entities. It's more manageable to pay back. It rewards profitable entities within the enterprise. It is more likely to get the creditors the full return on investment. It slows the bleed of job loss.

This is not an endorsement for a Communist takeover of corporations. These corporations have willingly availed themselves to the decisions of the state by filing for bankruptcy. The government is not seizing the assets, it's just reorganizing them to empower employees. Employee control over their enterprise is critical to the strength and vitality of a nation. Bankruptcy court is the perfect opportunity to curtail the negative influences of the American corporate aristocracy. If the billionaires and the multi-millionaires cannot manage their companies, their employees should at least get a chance to run it better. They are the ones who actually know their trade after all.

No safe harbor for American cash

Most of us do not have the luxury of offshoring our accounts in secretive tax shelters abroad. The United States typically turns a blind eye to this practice, and it is likely that many members of congress own offshore accounts, or have an interest in companies that do. It's such a common practice that it's not even concealed. Any half-competent business savvy person has cracked a joke about making a trip to Switzerland or taking a vacation to the Cayman Islands.

We know exactly where their money is. We know exactly which nations profit off of this behavior. We have a very strong idea about the quantity of assets stored there. Billions of dollars go untaxed every year. I have seen numbers as high as $22 trillion of untaxed wealth worldwide. While you and I struggle to come up with deductions to offset our 25% tax rate, the megacorporations and super-wealthy have yet another means of paying nothing.

There is a simple solution to this problem but it's very difficult to achieve politically. Most of these nations are small islands or city-states. The U.S. should ignore the tax shelter rules, and collect the tax anyway. This means we would have to tread on the national sovereignty of a tiny nation. It sounds bad, but we do it all the time for every other reason in the world with many large nations.

These nations have crafted policies specifically designed to screw the American public out of money, thereby robbing us of the value of our labor. All the things that we cannot afford are sitting in those tax-havens. All of the supposed deficits we have had while racking up trillions in national debt have been parked in offshore banks. Despite whatever mutual goodwill may exist between our nations, these countries have declared an economic war on the American people. It stands to reason then that we can use the force of our military to recover the people's money. We're perfectly comfortable imposing liability on corporations and people who sell certain goods to countries that we sanction. There is no reason we could not do the same for offshore accounts. Bank wherever you want, but you're still going to pay your fair share, or we'll come get it.

Most people in Congress are either super-wealthy themselves or in bed with the rich in some other capacity. Governments all over the world are stocked with billionaires who all have a vested interest in keeping these tax havens afloat. The joyous news is that in democratic nations all across the planet we outnumber them by an overwhelming majority. If your congressmen can't reign in offshore tax dollars, find one who can.

Democrats have previously at least made a modest effort towards recovering these lost funds during the Obama administration. I suggest that they start getting more aggressive about it. Instead of sliding it into a tax bill, it might be better to make it a big issue by giving it an independent bill. "The Offshore Tax Revenue Recovery of Act of 2021" is probably too boring to garnish the right amount of attention, so I might recommend something more glamorous like the "Stop the Tax Pirates Act" or the "Stop Fucking Over The Middle-Class Taxpayer Act". That has a much better ring to it, and it's definitely something you can take back and sell to your district. It would be so much fun to watch Mitch McConnell vote against that. As disingenuous as bill titles may be, it will still be entertaining to brand him as the pro-pirate, pro-taxfucker Senator when he scrambles to vote against it.

Capping Executive Wages

At the beginning of this section, I discussed the absurdity of the pay differential between a base level worker and a company CEO. This is not a problem that we can expect the market to resolve of its own accord. Incentive programs are unlikely to be significant enough to merit the necessary changes. Once the cat of greed is out of the bag, the only way you're going to put it back in is by the force of mandate.

Executive pay should be capped by a ceiling. The ceiling should not be determined by any set monetary value, but rather should be capped at a percentage relative to the company's lowest wage earners. We can tolerate a certain degree of compensation disparity and CEOs can still make the ungodly salaries they currently do. They just have to bring everyone else up with them. Maybe a modest 250% over, instead of a 1000% would be just fine.

A CEO should not be making millions, while its front-line workers make

$7.25 an hour. There's no economic justification for that whatsoever, and the government has a vested interest in correcting that. When social services are overburdened and the government is hemorrhaging money on anti-poverty programs, they need look no further than a CEO. Start sending them the bill. There's no reason why you and I should be paying for the CEO's of America to live high on a hog at the expense of their employees. That's just feudalism with a bow on it.

It should make us absolutely uncomfortable to endorse this behavior in the first place because it is an obvious evolution from the exploitative sharecropping of the past. No more kings, no more emperors, no more lords, and no more plantation owners. America was founded to get away from those people, and then we grew our own. It's time to depose the monarchy.

We are not your peasants. It amazes me to hear people who are otherwise incredibly poor defend the rights of a monarch to collect the wealth of their labor in the name of freedom. The argument is that the proletariat class of America could at any time through hard work pull itself up by its proverbial bootstraps to achieve the same thing. This is to ignore the fact that none of these people have been successful in doing so themselves. We call such a phenomenon the plight of the "temporarily embarrassed millionaire" voter. Vote for conditions as they exist for you today, not for conditions as you would want them to be if you were to suddenly win the lottery.

Are you a CEO making over 1000% more than a base-level employee? There is a statistical 99% probability that the answer is no. Not are you now, nor will you ever be in this position. Then why do we vote with such concern for their comfort and well being? Act as a tyrant, get deposed like a tyrant. Stop defending the billionaires. They'll be fine regardless, but if you do nothing, you won't be and neither will your neighbor.

Prioritize long term planning over short term capital gains.

The problem with corporations is ultimately that they are corporations. At the inception of a company, shares are usually held by members who have a deep personal connection to the business and are invested in its success. As the company becomes larger and the decades go by, they ultimately go public.

The more shareholders a corporation has who don't work for the corporation directly, the more difficult it is to stave off attacks on its profit margins.

It's a concept of business that is literally taught at universities. It's a truth of the business entity that is a corporation. All profits are for the shareholders. A good businessman thus maximizes shareholder profits. That sounds beautiful until you think about the size and integration of corporations in today's economy.

Despite better judgment, maximizing profits often means that you cut corners. You spend less on research and development. You spend less on advertising. You cut your employees and make the ones who remain work harder. You make cheaper lower quality products. You cut pay and benefits. Industry leaders will scoff at this statement because they believe that their company would never engage in this behavior. It only takes one committed majority shareholder to tank a corporation.

Today's impatient day traders bite companies like a bloodsucking vampire. They buy low. They loot the company to drive up share prices. The company looks successful. They sell high. The company crashes. Put that in a business textbook. The benevolent investor is often a proverbial unicorn.

Companies try to stave off hungry shareholders by paying out dividends. It's a great idea. It works for a while. Then they start demanding increases in those as well. The retention of value is not as important to them as growth. Our national investment strategy is built around the idea of growth above stability. It's not exactly a new idea. The Huns did it. The Romans did it. The Spaniards did it. The British did it. We know how empires fall, and we seem hellbent on being next in line.

There needs to be a safeguard against the tyranny of the short-term shareholder. It's no longer a matter of business, but rather a matter of national security. Our global competitors have discovered a simple means of ushering in our failing economy. They didn't have to build bombs. They just had to invest enough in our corporations to get voting power. They can extract our wealth without ever putting boots on our soil. They've also simultaneously discovered that they can use our own money to bankrupt us by buying up our real estate to artificially inflate property values. It's hardly what I would call Capitalism. Who owns our land? Who owns our money? Who owns our businesses? Who holds our manufacturing capacity by the balls? It's very obviously no longer the average working American and that's a huge problem.

The remedy to this situation is to strengthen the ownership capacity of employees. Employees with significant shareholder rights are the best line of defense against short-term decision making. The government should offer heavy tax subsidies and preferential treatment to U.S. owned and based worker-owned cooperatives and corporations that have a significant employee shareholder capacity.

Capital gains taxes are supposed to correct this problem, but it has very obviously not impacted this practice to any significant degree. If it has, then it is only evidence that much stronger measures are needed. There is a presumption that the 401K, 403B, IRA, or whatever investment tool corrects this problem. In my opinion, it only makes it worse. Sizable funds have strong ownership capacity, and they have a strong incentive to pursue constant growth. They have different risk classifications of course, but ultimately every fund in America is trying to squeeze out a solid 7% annual return rate. In fact, more and more Americans are relying on it for their retirement as Social Security becomes untenable. The problem is that continuous growth and improvement has a practical limit.

Most Americans are miserable and they hate their jobs. They feel over-worked and underpaid because they are. Constant work and constant critique have led to the decay of a nation. Our youth are stressed, depressed, and angry. We offer them very little consolation. Only the harsh realities that they will likely experience a lower standard of living than the generations which came before them. It should be obvious by now that our constant growth model is not going to result in greater prosperity or happiness.

That's because the theories of investment are entirely unreasonable. In order to sustain our economy in this environment, the entirety of the economy must average a forty-year growth rate of around 280%. In the average lifespan of an American, they are banking on a 560% increase in market conditions, not just for their livelihood, but also that it will continue to increase by the same rate or higher for the lifetime of all future generations.

Americans always seem so shocked by deep recessions without acknowledging that we set ourselves up for them. Who could have predicted the market crash of the Great Depression? Not the economist, nor owner, nor politician. The working man knows when the system is stressed beyond its limits. Recessions do not come about by natural cyclical causes. They occur because we built our capitalist economics around the idea of continuous expansion over stability and community.

I like to think of the economy as a neuron. If properly and ordinarily stimulated it will respond favorably and successfully to sustain normal biological functions. When you then start pumping your neurons full of cocaine you amplify the attenuation of the voltage curve. As your highs become higher, your lows become lower. Each successive time, you must take in more cocaine to achieve the same level or to exceed the previous level. Eventually, however, the stress on the system over-taxes its natural limits. The cell becomes unable to sustain normal function without it. It reaches an absolute maximum by which it can only decay when the amount of cocaine entering the system is saturated to the point that more of it no longer matters on a chemical basis. In the absence of cocaine, the cell begins to die, and once it dies, it cannot be mended.

We need an economy predicated on good sleep, diet, and exercise, but the economy we have is cocaine, meth, and heroine. Recessions do not have to be this damaging if you let the economy grow naturally. It cannot do so if we continue to prioritize short-term gains over long-term business strategies and sustainability. Let's take it back to a time when we just gave the economy some caffeine to wake up in the morning because right now it's facedown in an opioid den. We know this for certain, our economy cannot sustain even a two-week shutdown amidst a global pandemic without getting a major dose of stimulus. Admitting we have a problem is the first step in the battle.

The nature of our addiction rests in the disconnect of labor and policy. A community should own its community. Owners should also be operators. Employees should be shareholders. A king can sit in his castle in New York or San Francisco making unilateral decisions for a town that he has never once stepped foot in. His interests will never align with their own. Their labor becomes not for the betterment of themselves or the good of their community, but rather to support the lavish lifestyle of his majesty. In that sense, we have created microcosms of mercantilism in our country, whereby a handful of city-states now own the entirety of the productivity of the labor of his countrymen.

The purpose of democracy was meant to be a check on the rule of kings. We have a system by which the commoner is on an equal footing with the noblemen by virtue of the equality of his vote. If you take a walk down Mainstreet and find it boarded up by empty shops and dilapidated houses, owned by no one that you know, who lives in a faraway city, remind yourself that your community is empowered to do something about it. Private property is only as good as its use. You and your neighbors are only impoverished because you tolerate the rule of kings, but he has no true dominion over you. You are free to impose upon him the remedy of the electorate. Tax him away. Regulate him away. Adversely possess his property if it is not in use. Abolish his imminent domain. Reject his development proposals. Refuse to provide him with your labor. This requires an economy derived from the collective action of local citizens. Unify with those in your towns and neighborhoods to labor on behalf of each other. Make the goods and services with which you require. Buy from others in your neighborhood.

Otherwise, if this system continues unabated you will never restore vitality and stability to your community. Without strong communities, we lose our power as a nation. The government can support this in two ways. The first is getting out of the way and letting local people do what they need to do. The second is promoting ownership opportunities to give the common man the power of his own labor. We need leadership in Washington that shares this vision of property rights. Economic power is best distributed amongst the totality of the masses supplying the labor. The volume of the economy provided by government or by megacorporation is illusory and top-heavy.

Immigration Reform

- Build an economic wall.
- Amnesty for Dreamers.
- Accelerate processing of refugee applications.
- End the practice of immigration encampments.
- Reduce restrictions on visa applications.
- Resettle refugees in areas of the country experiencing population decline.

Another Brick in the Wall

Immigration policy is difficult. I've highlighted several areas throughout the text where immigration reform is desperately needed, but also unpopular. As a person who has lived in the ultimate border state for the greater part of thirty years I can tell you that most American's ideas about immigration are predicated on incredibly dated and ignorant ideas.

Democrats need to sit down for a moment and try to understand why people were willing to believe a man from New York who thought the best solution to illegal immigration was a physical barrier across the Mexican border. I can only surmise it is because they have no conception of our current immigration system and have never seen the border before.

The Wall is being built across a desert hellscape of rugged mountains, cacti, and the occasional melon patch. Ranchers have to have huge plots of land just to sustain cattle on it because the water and vegetation resources are so limited. This wall is being built along a river known to change its location continuously. Honestly, anyone who can make that trek across the desert and live deserves a medal. There is little need for a wall, and sections of the wall that they did build have already started to crack and fall over.

I have had numerous conversations with people in northern states about this. They are surprised that the southern counties of Texas keep trending Democrat. Wouldn't they want a wall to keep out all the *illegals*? The answer is not just no, but hell no. Many of our border fences and walls cross through the center of the most valuable ranch land in these border counties. Our obsession with physical barriers has ruined access to its most valuable resource, the river. Ranchers are rightfully mad as hell about the confiscation of their land. They could care less about the migrants crossing it. The government is far worse.

The presumption is that *illegal* immigrants are just walking across the border in migrating caravans. There are certainly people who do try to cross on foot every day, some of them successful. Most of them are not. The majority of people who become *illegals*, enter the country through a legitimate port of entry and then overstay their visa. For the past five years, Asian immigrants have been outpacing Mexican immigrants, and they didn't walk here. The wall was a pure work of fiction. It does nothing to address this issue.

If we are going to do anything at all about immigration-related issues, we should at least take action based on the facts as they exist in reality. The most common excuse for the imposition of some new crackdown on immigration is the idea of the undocumented criminal insurgent. It's a matter of national security they say. If we don't protect our borders, we'll never know who is here. It sounds like a meritorious argument, but when people enter lawfully on a visa, we do know who they are. They present a valid form of identification at the port of entry. We document who they are, where they came from, and where they're going. We even run them through a screening database. We know who these people are or at least have successfully presented themselves to be. No system is full-proof, but the U.S. is among the most stringent entry ports in the world.

I recall catching a red-eye flight to Barcelona. It was exhausting, and the plane was pretty no-frills. I didn't get an ounce of sleep. Our plane pulled into the furthest possible gate and dumped us out into a dark empty airport. After walking a few miles across the airport, we found ourselves in baggage claim. There was no entry gate, no checkpoints, no customs, no passport stamps. No one cared. Our driver was waiting for us and took us to the hotel. No one ever asked why we were there or where we were staying. Everyone was cordial and happy to take our money.

My experience made me wonder why anyone would want to *illegally* immigrate to the United States. We treat people like shit as they enter the country, legally or not. We look at them suspiciously once they are here. They're subjected to xenophobic and racist attacks. Most people here only speak one language. Then we tie our entire identity to our careers, as though there were nothing more to life than working. We've also replicated the same set of big-box stores so many times, most places look the same now.

Meanwhile, I'm walking down a pristine beach in Spain, enjoying the street vendor delights and the incredible architecture. People leave work during the middle of the day to spend time outdoors and take a nap. It's the only place I've ever seen people actively having sex on the beach, and among the few times I've been offered hard recreational drugs. For all the freedoms we purportedly enjoy, our nation is quite puritanical and oppressive. It may come as a shock to some Americans, but we're not exactly first on everyone's list for immigration. The people who are coming here, come because they really want to. We should honor that because they had options, but they chose to be here, to stay here, to live here, to work here, to spend money here.

There will always be nefarious people coming in as spies, or as part of criminal organizations, or those who seek to do us harm. Plenty of Americans are also involved in such activities. It's just one of those unfortunate facts of life. The wall is supposed to protect us from those people, but is it effective? We've poured a tremendous amount of money and resources into protecting our southern border, but our border with Canada remains wide open. Why don't we have a 5500-mile long wall to the north? That's because the wall was never about security. It's about money.

The perception is that Canada is safe. Most of them are wealthy enough.

They speak English. We're not worried about it. No one is putting up billions of dollars to build a wall across North Dakota to stop the migrant caravans of Canadians entering illegally. The irony is that Canadians are actually much better positioned to *steal* American jobs. What's keeping them up there? Why stay in Canada instead of coming over here?

It's about the differences in economic opportunity. The underlying causes of mass immigration stem from crises. People flee their countries for any number of reasons. War, famine, political upheaval, and persecution are fairly common. However, the most common reason is economic opportunity and infrastructure. People don't leave Canada because they are not in crisis and have no economic incentive to leave.

People cross the border from Mexico in pursuit of a better life for themselves and their families. That is our perception, but if we only look at this in isolation we miss the totality of the circumstances. Americans are also engaged in mass migratory patterns across state lines in pursuit of economic opportunity. That's why we see cities in the Midwest shrinking, while cities in the Southwest are expanding. These pathways have become so common that there is a legitimate campaign in Texas to stop the Californians from moving there, as though they were somehow a foreign invader encroaching on our sovereignty. Are we not all Americans? This is just a natural behavior of humans.

There is one particular place on the American border that merits discussion. The city of Presidio, Texas is a town of about 4,000 people that sits across the border from the Mexican city of Ojinaga, a city of about 28,000 people. What I find so fascinating about this arrangement is that there are actually more economic opportunities on the Mexican side of the border. Americans regularly cross the border to pursue employment opportunities in Mexico. There is more infrastructure and amenities on the Mexican side, and wages are relatively comparative relative to the cost of living expenses. The difference is that when we cross the border into Mexico, they're much friendlier to us than we are to them.

The narrative is always that *the Mexicans are coming to take your jobs!* The reality is that Americans are giving theirs away. Industry titans have stacked the border full of former U.S. factories for the affordability of labor and fewer regulations. They ship parts across the border, import the rest from Asia via the port of Houston, and send it to San Antonio for final assembly. That is the repercussion of our free trade agreements.

Here's the part of Mexico that you do not see. When I lived in San Marcos, I would witness hundreds of buses lining up at the outlet mall. While most Americans have shifted their purchasing habits to online sales, Mexicans still buy in-store retail. They come across the border and buy up tons of designer American clothing and take it back to Mexico for resale in boutiques. There are poor, wealthy, and middle-class people in both countries. It's not a one-way street like you are programmed to believe.

In my first year of teaching, I had a student who had just transferred in from Ojinaga. He had never been to an American school before. He spoke English as well as anyone else in the class. He received an advanced commendation on all of the standardized tests, that many American kids cannot even pass. His family was not wealthy. His parents never would have qualified for anything more than a temporary work visa and he would not have either. He had his share of personal problems, just like any other American kid, and ended up dropping out of high school. He is now a multi-millionaire, living a rockstar lifestyle in Los Angeles. The government that would have never allowed him to stay in the country before, now gleefully bends over backward to keep his tax dollars in the United States. Instead of looking at Mexico as a place ridden with problems, we should view it as a place ripe with opportunity.

Instead of spending billions of dollars every year trying to build and maintain a pointless wall, we should put that money into expanding commerce and infrastructure in border cities in Mexico and along our border. The border should be a highly attractive point of commerce where people on both sides flow back and forth, not the fortress walls of a warzone. People don't leave Canada because they have no reason to go anywhere else. If you want to stop the annual flow of *illegal* immigrants from Mexico, the best way to do that is to give people a reason to stay in Mexico.

It sounds bad on paper. Investing in Mexico sounds like an abuse of our tax dollars at work, but that is only because we are not focused on long term strategic planning. If we can elevate the economic conditions of the border communities, we can actualize massive cost savings from reduced need for border enforcement. If everything you need is right there, you're not going to risk your life crossing the desert. When cities on the border become mirror images of each other, commerce between the nations can increase. That means more buses of Mexicans coming into the United States spending money in our stores, paying our sales taxes, creating jobs right here at home. Improving the standing of border communities also makes it less lucrative to relocate American factories there. If the cost is the same either way, why mess with all the import-export hassle? There's a reason why American factories aren't rushing to the Canadian side of the border. When your neighbors are doing well, you're doing well.

If more Americans went to the Mexican border they would get a better semblance for what the needs are between the two countries and where we can find mutually beneficial opportunities. Our people share many of the same values, particularly in Texas. They work hard, they're resilient, they're self-sufficient. If we are truly a capitalist nation, we should welcome them into our markets with open arms. Their money and their labor are just as good as anyone else's. I would rather they spend it right here in the United States.

Amnesty for Dreamers

Imagine that you grew up in America. It's the only country that you've ever known or been to. You went to school here. Your friends and family are here. It's the center of your world. Then as you enter your adolescent years you suddenly discover that you are different from your other friends. All the things that you've been working towards are not available to you. You're not a citizen. Your parents brought you over here before you could even walk. It was through no action of your own. Now you find out that the government could at any moment destroy your entire life. They can arrest you without cause. Incarcerate you in a concentration camp. Then deport you. Not just you, but your entire family. You have few job options. Your college scholarship opportunities are limited. Even getting your driver's license is a potential risk. If someone commits a crime against you, you won't call the police or seek redress in court. If you are injured you will not seek out care in a hospital. The risks are simply too high.

As a high school teacher, I get to witness these struggles in my students every day. It's horrible to watch. My best and brightest students are always undocumented immigrants almost without exception. Knowing that they will likely never get the opportunity to be the person they were meant to become is a tragedy of humanity and a disgrace to our nation. I see doctors, lawyers, engineers, innovators that the United States will never have. Instead, we condemn these kids to a life of poverty, identity struggle, and suffering.

We call these people *dreamers* because obtaining citizenship is practically a fantasy. They have few legitimate opportunities to obtain it. DACA is a bandaid on a problem that is decades in the making. It creates a temporary path to maintaining their existence in this country, but it does nothing to confer real citizenship. Initially, I thought it was promising, but over the past four years, I have questioned the motives of the program, wondering if in the wrong hands it becomes a registry for deportations.

My undocumented students make jokes about going to prestigious universities just so they can meet a White girl to marry for the papers. They laugh it off, but it's also a legitimate consideration. I have had others ask me to adopt them, only for me to tell them that they are too old. Adoptions have to be finalized before their 15th birthday for citizenship purposes. Adult adoptions for citizenship purposes are also prohibited. They could leave the country for a few years and apply for a visa, but there is a strong possibility it will be denied and they may never be let back in.

They were brought here through no fault of their own. They grew up here. They think of themselves as Americans. They want to become fully contributing members of our society. Yet we provide them perhaps the fewest opportunities for any citizenship group. I have seen great young people crumble under the pressure. Seeing no way forward and having few options, they sink into a deep depression, they give up, or they look toward criminal enterprises as a means of economic sustenance.

Imagine that you are at school and you get a call that your entire family has been deported. You cannot go home. You also cannot stay here. Otherwise, you will also be deported to a country that you never knew. Our immigration laws cause more harm than they do good, and in my opinion, constitute an abuse of human rights in some circumstances.

We know who these kids are. They're just like any other American kids. It's not hard to just craft a law that confers a citizenship pathway for *dreamers*. The reluctance is entirely political, and until people come to see them as human beings the way that I do, such a bill will be almost impossible to pass.

Recognizing the political implications of this problem, Republican President Ronald Reagan passed a bill that provided stricter immigration controls, but also provided a nationwide blanket amnesty policy. This was a strategic economic decision, rather than one of moral significance. Undocumented immigrants have always been a popular choice among exploitative employers. They can get away with paying them significantly lower wages, and if they do it just right, they avoid paying taxes on that labor as well. Reagan knew that the United States could not deport three million people, and surely we know that we cannot deport the eleven million that we have today. However, if you are a U.S. citizen, you become traceable in the economy and must at least be paid minimum wage.

If you make them citizens, the U.S. gets to collect taxable income. The IRCA then imposes penalties on companies that employ *illegal* immigrants going forward. This meant that the 3 million workers who were previously undercutting American workers, were no longer able to do so and it brought them into direct competition. In that sense, legalization is actually more helpful to the American worker than just allowing perpetual undocumented labor to go unaddressed.

We currently have an estimated 11 million people living outside the system in a dark horse economy. Even with our stringent border controls and new agencies. Even with the fences and walls. Even with the technology. There is still a huge demand for under-the-table labor. Republicans like to talk about them as though they would be 11 million welfare recipients if given access to the system. What about the 11 million tax evaders currently undercutting the domestic labor market? Which is a bigger concern? The thought that 11 million more people could go on social services, programs that we already ignore and grotesquely underfund anyway, or the lost tax revenue from 11 million people?

The impact of blanket amnesty in 2020 would be huge. It would essentially bring in a potential income tax base the size of the state of Ohio. It would penalize the employers of undocumented immigrants far more than IRCA fines would because then they would have to pay their employees a fair wage.

It would also represent a huge prize for the political party that successfully granted it. While it is unlikely that all 11 million would become naturalized citizens, several million would. Those citizens would then be able to vote in elections. Every Hispanic Republican I know votes that way because of what happened in 1986. Democrats have the opportunity to capture a massive new voting block. While blanket amnesty may be politically unsavory, amnesty for *dreamers* is significantly more palatable from a talking points perspective. I think it is a realistic policy objective for Democrats to pursue, particularly if they explain the economic perspective of raking in the lost tax basin. They can also use talking points from DACA requirements, that these are working or college-educated kids who grew up in America who have no criminal record. The risk of social services drain is minimal when stacked against the potential tax revenue.

Treatment of Refugees

There is an old adage to do unto others as you would have done unto you. If that is a mantra to be lived by, the United States will find itself horribly mistreated in the event of a crisis. If unspeakable tragedy befalls our nation, who in the world will be willing to take us in? Will we languish in border encampments? Will we be imprisoned? Will we have to live in a constant state of instability as we wait years for the courts to process our applications?

You do not wake up one day and decide that you want to apply for refugee status. Something terrible has to happen for things to become so bad that you come to the border of a foreign country, leaving everything behind, and surrender yourself to an asylum process. When the makers of history judge the goodwill of our nation, I hope that it will show in times of crisis we used our wealth and advantages to help those in need when they most needed it.

The Trump administration has proven to be incredibly hostile towards refugees, and we've seen some horrific outcomes. Separating children from their families for no reason. Making refugees wait in their home countries or encampments in often dangerous conditions until their asylum is granted. Incarcerating refugees in prison-like concentration camps. There are no positive results of any of these policies. They only stand to kick a man when he is down.

If we are truly a capitalist nation, we would see the opportunity in refugee resettlement. The opportunity for new markets and new developments is tremendous. Particularly among those who have nothing left to lose. When people sit in waiting with impending uncertainty, they only cost money. The longer they languish in refugee camps and government limbo, the less likely they will be to financially or socially recover.

There have been some highly successful refugee resettlement efforts in the United States. One of the best ideas I have seen in recent years is placing refugees in economically depressed areas of the country that are experiencing population declines. One such example is the relocation of Bhutanese refugees to Akron, Ohio. This has been a tremendous boost to the city as it was in the process of undergoing a major population loss. It has helped fill empty homes and restore commercial vitality to shuddered businesses. They may not have started out with much money, but they are quickly becoming a thriving and expanding tax base. When integrated into the community, refugees tend to reward the cities that take them in, particularly in the second generation. This is in part because they do not come here just to work. They come here to be free and to build a new life of strength and vitality. Instead of letting able-bodied skilled labor waste away in prison camps, we should be putting them to work in rebuilding our declining metropolitan areas all throughout the nation.

Here in Arlington, we have managed to actualize tremendous economic value from taking in refugee populations. We have a thriving Vietnamese and Thai community here that has generated hundreds of small businesses since their arrival. We have been strengthened by their contributions over the decades and enjoy a wide array of goods and services otherwise unavailable, from Asian markets to quality restaurants serving a diverse pallet. Where else can you get Vietnamese food and tacos in the same store? Our local university is heavily supported by international students from India and we have seen subsequent commercial opportunities emerge from this exchange as well. I certainly have never heard any of our local politicians complain about the tax revenues or development that they have provided.

We should accelerate these refugee status applications, so we can get these people out in the economy as quickly as possible where they are needed the most. We should also broaden the strict requirements on qualifications for refugee status to address modern American values. The current requirements exclude many people who should otherwise be included if we consider the circumstances under which their life is being jeopardized by conditions or laws of their home countries. Sending someone back to their country to die is horrific, and if we have any standards of justice and morality, we would invest more in hearing the cry of freedom around the globe.

On that note, the very idea that we are separating families and holding people in crowded concentration camps is deeply disturbing. This is counter to every American value we claim to stand for. After the horrific abuses suffered by victims of the Holocaust during the Nazi occupation, I cannot believe that any policymaker in Washington would ever consider recreating those conditions here. These temporary immigration holding cells are emerging in much the same way, and are in my opinion only steps away from becoming them. There are literally children dying of negligent care in these facilities. The camps are purposefully frequently relocated to make it more difficult for watchdog agencies to find out what is happening inside. As more reports come out, we find that physical and sexual abuse in these encampments is rampant. As far as I am concerned we are only a few bad decisions away from becoming the next epicenter of genocide. This practice must be stopped immediately.

Our immigration courts are kept deliberately slow. There are not enough judges to support the volume of cases. Many of the cases are mismanaged and contain little in the way of proper evidence, due process, or any regard for human decency. It is perhaps the most disturbing event in judicial history that children as young as three years old are ordered to appear in court unattended to their own deportation proceedings. It's sickening and I do not understand why we tolerate the existence of these kangaroo courts or these encampments.

During the height of misinformation, a flash campaign arose in 2020 predicated on the idea that high profile Democratic politicians ran a child trafficking operation. People quickly rallied to the defense of the non-existent children without any regard for the facts behind the baseless unfounded accusations. They could be seen lining the streets holding signs and screaming "save the children." Save the children indeed. Why are more Americans willing to rally to the support of fictitious children in a manufactured slander campaign, but refuse to acknowledge the plight of real children in the custody of our immigration system? The answer perhaps rests in feelings of guilt. They protest something false to avoid having to actually do something about reality.

If I were a Democratic politician I would be following those camps every-where they moved. Everyone in my district would know what was happening there every day. Every judge would be made to answer for unaccompanied minors in their courtrooms. I would dismantle the entire agency and start over again. Voting to impeach the President on a minor technicality, and calling him a fascist is the save-the-children equivalent of governing. There is a difference between protesting something fictitious and taking action on something real. Be the party that takes action on something real.

Win First, Take the High Ground Later: Reclaiming Labels and Cleaning House

- Reclaim the narratives.
- Keep your distance from the bandwagon.
- Don't eat your own.
- Sharpen your fangs.
- Ineffective leadership needs to be replaced.

This is not as much a policy issue as it is a strategic one. Remember back when you were a kid and your parents would spout off a list of off-limit topics and behaviors for your visit to grandma's house? It probably went something like this: "she's old and doesn't know any better" or "try to keep the peace" or "you know how they feel about this or that issue". In fact, it has been the norm not to discuss politics at the Thanksgiving dinner table for decades now. Except that isn't really what it was, was it? Your conservative relatives talked politics all the live-long day, while you quietly smiled and nodded into your wine glass. Somehow you allowed grandma's fragile sense of morality to railroad you into silence. Pardon my French grandma, but fuck that!

I look back with regret on times when I ought to have said something. My great aunt was a dear old southern woman. Nothing but sweet tea. Prim and proper. Never one to ruffle feathers. However, she couldn't encounter a Black man in the grocery store without somehow commenting on his race by using the N-word, as though it were a term of endearment. How difficult would it have been for me to say "his race is unimportant to this story" or "let's not use that word anymore." As an old man, I hope with all sincerity that my grandchildren call me out on my own bullshit. Just because you are old or because you are conservative does not give you the right to be an ignorant jackass. The same is true for the Republican party.

I've watched idly by as the Democratic party quietly let the Republicans hijack God in the name of their branding. It's frankly disgusting. We have normalized the use of the GOP as "God's Own Party," an old joke here in the South that really isn't funny. The idea that a political party is allowed to claim God in the name of policy is inherently anti-American. The very first amendment of our Constitution is designed to prohibit the political imposition of religious philosophy and it's time that Democrats restore respect to that institution. The next time a Republican says what they think God wants, you clap back and say what you think God wants. It's only fair. We've seen Republican Jesus evolve into a monstrous creature that endorses war, hates the LGBT community, shuns helping the sick and the poor, and turns a blind eye to sexism. Feel free to say something about it. Their interpretation of the Bible is just as valid as yours. Great Grandma has no more right to her sensibilities than you do, so let her have it!

I have seen Republicans do the same thing with gun rights. How many times have you seen "the Democrats are coming to take your guns!" work as a marketing strategy? They hit us with that all the time. Then you get a smartass like Beto O'Rourke who feeds the flames with a "hell yes we're going to take your AR-15s." In Texas especially, Republicans are genuinely fearful that the Democrats are going to confiscate their guns and march them off to Communist reeducation camps. I wish I was kidding, but that's the mantra that I hear over and over again. My Republican friends are so captivated by that narrative, they actually believe that Democrats don't own guns. Nothing could be further from the truth.

Growing up in my neighborhood just about every kid on the block had a BB-gun. Their parents had at least a .22 caliber rifle and a 12-gauge shotgun. Occasionally, we would go out to someone's land to hunt deer or fowl. Somehow they forgot that all their Democrat friends were a part of that same fabric. Almost every Democrat I know owns a gun, if not multiple guns. They tend to own handguns, while Republicans are more likely to own long-guns and semi-automatics. The difference is that Democrats don't go parading around town waving their guns in the air like a dumbass. For a group of people who are so fearful about the government coming to take their guns, Republicans do a fantastic job of showing everyone how many they have and where they are located.

That needs to be the narrative on guns. Ownership isn't partisan. It's about sensible and responsible use. Just another example of Republicans controlling the narrative. Democrats need to tell their own story without getting a rewrite from the opposing party and without getting censured by their own. If you want Southern Democrats to win elections, you have to allow them to say what they need to say and support the policy that they need to support. There are certain issues in certain states that you just won't get movement on. Sometimes you have to lose a few battles to win the war.

On the other hand, Democrats also need to stop jumping on the "cancel-culture bandwagon" as it's become known. The formation of labels is counterproductive. The more you brand legislation towards a particular label, the less buy-in you are going to get for that policy. Design policy because it is a good policy. If it happens to strongly benefit one group over another, then so be it. When we say "this bill is for *this* group" we alienate the other groups, and we create Republicans out of voters in other groups that would have also benefited from the legislation had we passed it more broadly.

Democrats have allowed themselves to be branded. Republicans say that Democrats are liberal, that they are the out of control spenders when they are the ones who rack up the deficits the most. Republicans call any policy they dislike socialist or Communist because they know Americans fear those terms and are ignorant about them. Republicans now also proclaim themselves as the holders of truth, whereby they can fabricate any lie they want, and make it a reality. It's reached the height of hubris with voters genuinely believing in the existence of lizard people. I wish that was a lie, but the bullshit has continued long enough. All I am going to say is that it's time for Democrats to aggressively set the record straight, and frankly do some "truth-telling" of their own. Washington didn't win the Revolution by fighting fair.

Keep your candidates positive and on message, but behind the scenes, the Democrats need attack dogs of their own, and no Rachel Maddow doesn't count. Republicans will go to any length to win, as we've seen play out to an absurd degree in the desperate attempt by the Trump administration to suppress the vote and supplant the electorate. What are Democrats willing to do? Americans don't fault you for the scandal, they fault you for the weakness. Own up to shit and stop apologizing for everything. Republicans never do and they still win.

On the other hand, we also can't be outraged about things the majority of Americans have never heard of and probably don't care about. While we certainly want a society that evolves and speaks freely on such matters, we also need to understand that not everyone is going to be on the same page about it at the same time. This doesn't mean you should keep it off the Thanksgiving dinner table, but maybe don't stab anyone with the carving knife over it. Democrats do this all the time and it tends to bite us in the ass at the ballot box.

An example of late is the emergence of multiplicitous gender terminology. While you have the right to label yourself whatever gender you want and live a life free of governmental discrimination, you also have to understand that the majority of Americans are entirely unfamiliar with it. It's not even a lack of education, it's that they genuinely have never even thought about it before. Even in the echelons of academic circles, most Americans are still not cognizant of neutral pronouns. It's just not part of their vernacular, and they've likely never met someone who does employ such terms. I understand this quest for acceptance and recognition is an uphill battle, but you have to give people time. It's not persuasive to get overly aggressive and angry about it. All that does is turn people off to your movement.

That is not to say you should remain silent when someone attacks you, but learn to separate those who hate you from those who just genuinely don't know or understand. Help people understand, speak out when you are attacked but have an end goal in mind. What is it that you really want from these people? If all you want to do is ruin their life, you're no better than those who seek to harm you in the same way.

I have seen Democratic politicians devour their own and call for the resignation of members of the party who make relatively minor gaffes. You don't see Republicans doing that. As wonderful as it is to take the moral high road, understand that the other party doesn't play by the rules. There are no points for second place. Almost winning an election, almost defeating a bill, almost passing a bill, almost blocking a judicial nominee, almost impeaching the President, is not the same as actually doing it. Do what is necessary to win again and sort out the infighting behind closed doors where party business used to be handled.

Some things to consider in times such as this; Has the person apologized for the problem? Has the person clarified or recanted a statement? Has the person's position evolved over time in light of new revelations? Accept that mistakes will be made and that humans are imperfect beings. Democrats so often bite the hand that feeds them when it comes to social minutia. Don't go destroying someone's life over a minor issue, when the bulk of their efforts have supported you. Help them understand and grow instead.

I don't mean this in the sense of loyalty, I just ask that you examine the totality of the circumstances. Prioritize your political opponents. This ignorance plays out at the ballot box when voters write in bullshit candidates on principle, all because they didn't get everything they wanted. Hillary Clinton might have had some flaws, but in retrospect, I can't help but wonder how all those Bernie write-in voters felt about four years of the Trump administration. Mick Jagger said it best, "you can't always get what you want", and you're never going to get everything you want with politics. Make sure that voters understand how the process works. You have to vote and legislate within reality. Until you have changed reality, voting for a fantasy is a wasted vote. Incremental change is almost always better than nothing.

This also includes putting that philosophy into practice. Good governance must continue. Democrats and Republicans are going to have to work together to pass bills. There is never going to be something that everyone fully agrees on, but we can get pretty close. While our system of elections says we only need to please 50.1% of the electorate, let's remember that the 49.9% are still there, and their needs are still valid. If a bill doesn't strike a solid majority with your district, don't vote on it. If it's a good policy, the people who voted for you and the people who didn't vote for you will agree with it. Unfortunately, I don't see Republicans making the effort either, so I'm not sure what the best way forward is, but we need to do something.

One suggestion I have is to stop putting the same people in charge when things aren't working. I'm going to go out on a limb here and say Nancy and Mitch are not the best choices. Clearly, they cannot work together. Let's give someone else a try. Democrats should cut a deal with moderate sensible Republicans in the Senate. How many Democrats and Republicans would it take to make Mitt Romney the senate majority leader instead? How about Susan Collins? They're not ideal, but they're infinitely better than Mitch. Nancy Pelosi is equally abrasive and a turnoff to most Americans. I'm sure she does great fundraising and has had a long distinguished career in the party, but after our losses in 2010, she never should have come back to the gavel. Give someone else a chance to get it done. Trying the same ideas and the same people over and over again expecting to achieve new results has only led to stagnation and frustration.

They say that we live in Red states and Blue states, but we see the winds of change. The boundaries of our districts are about to be redrawn again in light of the new Census. It's time for ideas to change as well. We need a fresh slate of politicians with modern perspectives. We need a Democratic Party that casts a wide tent not because it is urban, but because it represents the average everyday American. We need a government that works for the good of the nation, not just half of it. Out with the old, and in with the blue.

The New Blue.

Acknowledgements and Accreditations

There are few original ideas. You will find these policies endorsed and echoed across the political landscape. If it all sounds similar, it is only because reasonable people have made the same observations and come to the same conclusions. That being said, there are several works of great influence to this work that deserve acknowledgement. Think of them as options for further reading.

Should you find any of my policy recommendations or presentation of ideas to be in error, I would be happy to hear the merits of your claim. My pride is not so important that I cannot admit to my mistakes. Hopefully, even in the moments where I am wrong, I have at least sparked deeper conversation and civil discourse on the issues. The moment that we blockade ourselves from the influence of persuasion in light of new facts, is the moment that we have stopped learning. Present your research findings to the contrary and I will give consideration to your arguments and I hope that you will give me the same courtesy.

Boortz, N., & Linder, J. (2009). *The Fair Tax Book: Saying Goodbye to the Income Tax and the IRS*. New York: HarperCollins e-books.

Burdick, J. F. (2016). *Talking about single payer: Health care equality for America*. St. Michaels, MD: Near Horizons Publishing.

Buttigieg, P. (2020). *SHORTEST WAY HOME: One mayor's challenge and a model for america's future*. S.l.: JOHN MURRAY LT.

Carter, J. (2007). *Our endangered values: America's moral crisis*. Waterville, Me.: Large Print Press.

Curl, J., Reed, I., & Curl, J. (2012). *For all the people: Uncovering the hidden history of cooperation, cooperative movements, and communalism in America.* Oakland, CA: PM Press.

Dray, P. (2011). *There is power in a union: The epic story of labor in America.* NY, NY: Anchor Books.

Desmond, M. (2016). *Evicted: Poverty and profit in the American city.* New York: Crown.

Dolan, T. J. (2017). *Molten salt reactors and thorium energy.* Duxford, United Kingdom: Woodhead Publishing, an imprint of Elsevier.

Dufton, E. (2017). *Grass roots: The rise and fall and rise of marijuana in America.* New York: Basic Books.

Hoffman, A. (2016). *An Intimate Conversation with my Younger Self.* : CreateSpace Independent Publishing Platform.

Frank, T. (2005). *What's the matter with Kansas?: How conservatives won the heart of America.* New York: Henry Holt.

Grann, D. (2018). *Killers of the Flower Moon: The Osage Murders and the Birth of the FBI.* New York: Vintage Books, A Division of Penguin Random House LLC.

Gross-Loh, C. (2014). *Parenting without borders.* New York: Penguin Group.

Ledbetter, J. (2011). *Unwarranted influence: Dwight D. Eisenhower and the military-industrial complex.* New Haven: Yale University Press.

Lewis, J. (2016). *Across that bridge: Life lessons and a vision for change.* New York: Hachette Books.

Locke, J. (1952). *The second treatise of government.* Indianapolis: Bobbs-Merrill.

Louv, R. (2013). *Last Child in the Woods: Saving our Children from Nature-Deficit Disorder.* London: Atlantic Books.

Lydon, M., Garcia, A., & Duany, A. (2015). *Tactical urbanism: Short-term action for long-term change.* Washington, DC: Island Press.

Obama, B. (2008). *Change we can believe in.* Canongate Books.

Olivas, M. A. (2020). *Perchance to Dream: A Legal and Political History of the Dream ACT and Daca.* New York University Press.

Marohn, C. L. (2020). *Strong towns: A bottom-up revolution to rebuild*

American prosperity. Hoboken, NJ: John Wiley & Sons.

Marx, Karl, 1818-1883. (1959). *Das Kapital, a critique of political economy.* Chicago :H. Regnery,

Parolek, D. G., & Nelson, A. C. (2020). *Missing middle housing: Thinking big and building small to respond to today's housing crisis.* Washington, DC: Island Press.

Perot, R. (1992). *United we stand: How we can take back our country.* New York: Hyperion.

Perry, H. W. (1994). *Deciding to decide: Agenda setting in the United States Supreme Court.* Cambridge, MA: Harvard University Press.

Regan, J., & Smith, C. (2019). *Agrarian reform and resistance in an age of globalisation: The Euro-American world and beyond, 1780-1914.* London: Routledge.

Rothstein, R. (2018). *The color of law: A forgotten history of how our government segregated America.* New York: Liveright Publishing Corporation, W.W. Norton & Company.

Tocqueville, Alexis de, (1838). *Democracy in America.* New York, G. Dearborn & Co.

Yang, A. (2019). *The war on normal people: the truth about America's disappearing jobs and why universal basic income is our future.* New York, NY: Hachette Books.

Zehr, H. (2016). *The little book of restorative justice.* Vancouver, B.C.: Langara College.

Zweede-Tucker, Y. (2012). *The meat goat handbook: Keeping goats for food, profit and fun.* Minneapolis: Voyageur.